DK SMITHSONIAN HANDBOOKS
GEMSTONES

SMITHSONIAN HANDBOOKS
GEMSTONES

CALLY HALL

Photography by
HARRY TAYLOR
(Natural History Museum)

Editorial Consultant
JOSEPH J. PETERS

A Dorling Kindersley Book

3032858664

LONDON, NEW YORK, MUNICH,
MELBOURNE, and DELHI

Project Editor Alison Edmonds
Project Art Editor Alison Shackleton
Series Editor Jonathan Metcalf
Series Art Editor Spencer Holbrook
Production Controller Caroline Webber
U.S. Consultant Joseph J. Peters
U.S. Editor Charles A. Wills

First American Edition, 1994
Reprinted with corrections in 2000
Second American Edition, 2002
10

Published in the United States by
Dorling Kindersley, Inc.
375 Hudson Street
New York, NY 10014

A Cataloging-in-Publication record
is available from the Library of Congress
ISBN 0-7894-8985-6

Computer page makeup by Adam Moore
Text film output by The Right Type, Great Britain
Reproduced by Colourscan, Singapore
Printed and bound by South China Printing Company in China

see our complete product line at
www.dk.com

CONTENTS

AUTHOR'S INTRODUCTION

The mysterious appeal of gemstones, their exquisite colors and the play of light within them, would alone have made them precious to many, but their rarity, hardness, and durability have made them doubly valuable. The natural beauty, strength, and resilience of gems have inspired beliefs in their supernatural origins and magical powers, and stones that have survived the centuries have gathered a wealth of history and romance around them.

THERE ARE OVER 3,000 different minerals, but only about 50 are commonly used as gemstones. Others are cut for collectors of the unusual but are not suitable for wear because they are too soft and easily scratched. The number of minerals commonly used as gemstones constantly changes as new sources and varieties are found and fashions change. Over 130 gem species, including some exceptionally rare stones, are described in this book, illustrating the very wide range of naturally occurring gemstones.

SORTING SAPPHIRES
Workers in Myanmar (Burma) sort through sapphires collected from river sediment. When cut, they epitomize the allure of gemstones.

WHAT IS A GEMSTONE?

To be regarded as a gemstone, a mineral (or occasionally an organic material) must be beautiful, most importantly in its color.

RIVER PEARL (UNCUT)

STAR SAPPHIRE (CABOCHON)

DIAMOND (BRILLIANT CUT)

FIVE MAJOR GEMSTONES
These five stones are the most highly prized. All except pearl have a particular cut that brings out their best qualities.

RUBY (STEP CUT)

EMERALD (OCTAGONAL CABOCHON)

A gemstone must also be durable – hard enough to survive constant use or handling without becoming scratched or damaged. Finally, it must be rare, because its very scarcity endows it with a greater market value.

THE SCIENCE OF GEMOLOGY

Gems are scientifically fascinating, too. Gemologists make a complete study of each stone they acquire, both as it is found in rocks and after it has been cut and polished. That is why the species entries in this book show the gem in its rough, natural state, perhaps still embedded in the host rock (or matrix),

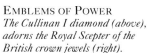
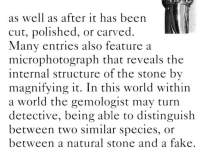

EMBLEMS OF POWER
The Cullinan I diamond (above), adorns the Royal Scepter of the British crown jewels (right).

as well as after it has been cut, polished, or carved. Many entries also feature a microphotograph that reveals the internal structure of the stone by magnifying it. In this world within a world the gemologist may turn detective, being able to distinguish between two similar species, or between a natural stone and a fake.

KINGS AND COMMONERS

Throughout the ages, gemstones have been seen as representations of wealth and power. Symbols of supremacy, from crowns to richly decorated robes, have traditionally been adorned with jewels. But

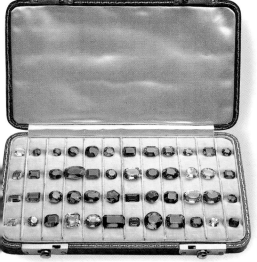

PRIVATE COLLECTION
The Mathews collection in London comprises 4 boxes of unmounted gems from all around the world (above), and a group of Colombian emeralds (right). The scope of this collection is unique, but many fine examples of cut and uncut gemstones are on public display in museums.

gemstones are not just for the wealthy or the scientifically minded: they can be appreciated by anyone, from the amateur gem-spotter to the enthusiast who enjoys their beauty and history. For this reason, the *Eyewitness Handbook of Gemstones* is not intended as a textbook but as a general introduction and an initial guide to identification.

COLLECTING GEMS

For many, the real satisfaction comes from actually owning gems. Most people cannot afford the more

A BOX OF JEWELS
In the 18th century, jeweled trinkets like this decorative box were very fashionable. A large citrine is in the center, surrounded by amethyst, agates, amazonite, garnet, and pearls.

MINING IN CAMBODIA
In many parts of the world, traditional methods and equipment are still employed for the collection of gemstones.

expensive stones, but anybody can collect a few minerals that, even if not gem quality, are still very attractive. You may even chance on a piece of amber on a beach, or come across a beautiful piece of jewelry in a local auction. No matter how modest your collection, it will give you hours of fascination and enjoyment.

FOSSICKING IN AUSTRALIA
Fossicking (foraging) for sapphires and opals is still possible in parts of Australia, as long as you first obtain a permit from the authorities. River beds and streams are the best locations.

HOW THIS BOOK WORKS

THIS BOOK is divided into three parts: precious metals, cut stones, and organics. Cut stones are arranged by crystal structure into seven groups (cubic, tetragonal, hexagonal, trigonal, orthorhombic, monoclinic, and triclinic), but with a final section on amorphous gems. Within these sections, gem species are grouped with other species of a similar mineralogical type. The page below explains a typical entry.

crystal group to which gem belongs •

basic chemical composition of gem •

mean hardness of gem, measured on Mohs scale •

Crystal structure Trigonal	Composition Silicon dioxide	Hardness 7

gem's common • name, with mineral group in brackets (when appropriate)

AMETHYST (QUARTZ)

Crystalline quartz in shades of purple, lilac, or mauve is called amethyst, a stone traditionally worn to guard against drunkenness and to instill a sober and serious mind. Amethyst is dichroic, showing a bluish or reddish purple tinge when viewed from different angles. Usually faceted as a mixed or step cut, amethyst has distinctive inclusions that look like tigerstripes, thumbprints, or feathers. Some amethyst is heat treated to change the color to yellow, producing citrine (see opposite). Crystals that are part citrine and part amethyst are called ametrine.

gem's chief • physical characteristics

• OCCURRENCE Amethyst is found in alluvial deposits or in geodes. Some of the largest geodes containing amethyst are in Brazil. Amethyst from the Urals (Russia) has a reddish tinge; Canadian amethyst is violet. Other localities include Sri Lanka, India, Uruguay, Madagascar, the USA, Germany, Australia, Namibia, and Zambia.

where and • how gem formed, and where it is found

• REMARK Poor quality material is often tumbled into beads. If a stone is pale it may be set in a closed setting or have foil placed behind it to enhance the color. Amethyst has been imitated by glass and synthetic corundum.

additional • information relevant to gem species or type

closeup • photograph of inclusions in gem (if appropriate)

Characteristic tigerstripe inclusions are caused by parallel, liquid-filled canals.

TIE PIN
Amethyst jewelry was popular in the late 19th century. This handsome gold tie pin is adorned with an octagonal step-cut amethyst.

example of • jewelry or ornament included in some entries to illustrate use

typical purplish violet color

purple stone • from Russia

polished, convex front

alternate colors • due to twinning

example of • faceted gem, labeled with name of cut

OVAL MIXED CUT

other color • varieties and cuts shown to assist in identification

HEXAGONAL MIXED CUT

color darkens toward tip of • amethyst crystal

annotation • highlights key physical characteristics

slice cut • perpendicular to length of crystal

AMETHYST CRYSTAL SLICE

specimen of • gem as it occurs naturally, often shown in host rock (matrix)

faceting styles and shapes popular for this gem •

Baguette	Bead	Mixed

AMETHYST CRYSTALS ASSOCIATED WITH ROCK CRYSTAL

SG 2.65	RI 1.54–1.55	DR 0.009	Luster Vitreous

mean figure • for specific gravity of gem

mean range of refrac- • tive values (singly refractive gems have one mean value only)

mean value of • birefraction (doubly refractive gems only)

surface shine • or "look" of gem

WHAT ARE GEMSTONES?

GEMSTONES are generally minerals that have been, or may be, fashioned to use for personal adornment. As a rule, they are beautiful, rare, and durable. Most are minerals: natural, inorganic materials with a fixed chemical composition and regular internal structure.

A few gems, like amber and pearl, come from plants or animals and are known as organics. Others, called synthetics, do not have a natural origin but are made in laboratories. Their physical properties are similar to those of natural gems, and they may be cut to imitate the real thing.

PRECIOUS METALS

The precious metals are gold, silver, and platinum. They are not true gemstones, but they are attractive and easily worked and have their own intrinsic value, often as settings for gems. Platinum is the rarest and the most valuable.

POLISHED STONE
Crystals may be rounded and polished naturally (like this emerald pebble, rolled in a stream) or ground mechanically.

GOLD RING

GOLD NUGGET
(UNWORKED)

ORGANICS

Gem materials produced by living organisms are called organics. Their sources are as diverse as shellfish (which produce pearls), polyps (whose skeletal remains form coral), and the fossilized resin from trees (which makes amber). Ivory, jet, and shell are also organics. These materials are not stones and are not as durable as mineral gems. Instead of being faceted like mineral gems, they are usually polished or carved, or drilled and threaded as beads.

NATURAL CRYSTAL
In its natural state, the mineral may be a prism, with clearly defined faces.

CUT STONES

Like the emerald shown here, almost all cut gems begin life in a crystalline form (see pp.18–19), embedded in a host rock known as the matrix. In this state, the stone is referred to as a rough. Many natural crystals are attractive enough to be displayed as they are. Others are faceted and polished to enhance their beauty (see pp.26–29), then set in a piece of jewelry or an ornament.

AMBER BEAD

AMBER ROUGH

CABOCHON
A simple fashion for stones is to cut them en cabochon, *producing a domed, highly polished surface.*

**IMITATION EMERALD
(GARNET ON GLASS)**

FACETED STONE
Most gemstones are cut to give them a number of flat surfaces, called facets. The facets absorb and reflect light, to magical effect.

IMITATIONS
Gemstones have been imitated throughout the ages. Many lesser stones have been used, as well as glass paste and other manmade materials. Composite stones, like the red garnet on green glass (above), are made of more than one piece.

JEWELRY
A piece of jewelry, usually one or several polished or faceted stones set in a mount of precious metal, is often the finished product.

SYNTHETICS
Manmade synthetic stones (see pp.34–35) are similar in chemical composition and optical properties to their natural equivalents. In the flux method, crystals are grown, then faceted (right).

**SYNTHETIC
CRYSTALS**

**SYNTHETIC
FACETED EMERALD**

How Gemstones Are Formed

GEMSTONES THAT HAVE a mineral origin are found in rocks or in gem gravels derived from these rocks. Rocks themselves are made up of one or more minerals and may be divided into three main types. The formation of these three types – igneous, sedimentary, or metamorphic – is a continuous process, described in terms of the rock cycle (shown right). Gem-quality minerals within these rocks may be easily accessible at the Earth's surface or lie buried deep beneath it. Others, separated from their host rock by erosion, are carried by rivers to lakes or the sea.

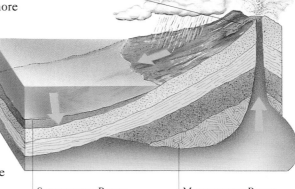

IGNEOUS ROCKS
form as molten rock solidifies, above or below ground. This erodes and is deposited as sediments. •

• SEDIMENTARY ROCKS
are formed from the accumulation and compression of eroded rock fragments. They may eventually be buried back below the surface.

• METAMORPHIC ROCKS
may be either sedimentary or igneous rocks whose character is fundamentally changed by heat and pressure.

peridot crystals form as lava cools •

VOLCANIC BOMB FORMED FROM BASALTIC LAVA

METAMORPHIC ROCKS
Metamorphic rocks are either igneous or sedimentary rocks that have been changed by heat and pressure within the Earth to form new rocks with new minerals. As this happens, gemstones can grow within them. Garnets, for example, form in rocks called mica schists, which were once mudstones and clays. Marble, formed from limestone that has been subjected to intense pressure and high temperatures, may contain rubies.

IGNEOUS ROCKS
Igneous rocks have solidified from molten rock, which comes from deep beneath the Earth's surface. Some, called extrusive igneous rocks, are thrown out from volcanoes as lava, volcanic bombs (see left), or ash. Intrusive igneous rocks are those that solidify beneath the surface. Essentially, the slower a rock cools and solidifies, the larger the crystals – and therefore the gemstones – formed within it. Many large gemstone crystals form in a kind of intrusive igneous rock known as pegmatite.

kyanite and staurolite crystals form under high pressure •

KYANITE-STAUROLITE SCHIST

SEDIMENTARY ROCKS

Sedimentary rocks are formed by the accumulation of rock fragments produced by weathering. In time, these fragments settle down and harden into rock once more. Sedimentary rocks are usually laid down in layers, and these may be shown as a feature in decorative stones. Most Australian opal occurs in sedimentary rocks; turquoise occurs mainly as veins in sedimentary rocks such as shale; halite and gypsum *are* sedimentary rocks.

blue-green opal in veins and fissures

AUSTRALIAN OPAL IN SEDIMENTARY ROCK

ORGANIC GEMS

Organic gems come from plants and animals. Natural pearls form around foreign bodies that have made their way inside the shells of marine or freshwater shellfish. Cultured pearls are produced artificially in large fisheries, many in the shallow waters off the shores of Japan and China. Shells treated as gems may come from animals as diverse as snails and turtles, living in the ocean, in fresh water, or on land. Coral is made up of the skeletons of tiny marine animals called coral polyps. Bone, or ivory from the teeth or tusks of mammals, may come from recently living animals or from fossils thousands of years old. Amber is fossilized tree resin, collected from soft sediments or the sea. Jet is fossilized wood, found in some sedimentary rocks.

TREASURE FROM THE SEA
The action of seawater has given this piece of amber (fossilized tree resin), washed up on a beach in Norfolk, England, a pitted and worn surface.

MODERN DIAMOND MINE IN BOTSWANA
Some gemstones are so valuable that large-scale mining, in which tons of rock may be extracted to collect tiny amounts of gemstone, are still viable.

ALLUVIAL MINING FOR SAPPHIRES
Small-scale mining with traditional methods and equipment, such as this in Sierra Leone, is still common in many countries.

WHERE GEMSTONES ARE FOUND

SOME GEM MINERALS, such as quartz and garnet, are found worldwide. Others, like diamonds and emeralds, are rarer, due to the more unusual geological conditions necessary for their formation. Even when a mineral is found worldwide, only a minute proportion may be of gem quality. The main gem localities of the world are therefore those where gem-quality material occurs in sufficient quantity to make production economical.

DIAMONDS OF AFRICA
The kimberlite rocks of southern Africa are mined in a modern, large-scale way, producing vast quantities of diamonds for both industrial and gem use.

Germany

Italy

United States

Mexico

Colombia

Brazil

Nige

Zamb

Botswan

South Afri

KEY TO SYMBOLS

DIAMOND	RUBY	SAPPHIRE	EMERALD
AQUAMARINE	CHRYSOBERYL	TOPAZ	TOURMALINE
PERIDOT	GARNET	PEARL	OPAL

TWELVE KEY GEMS
The 12 varieties of gemstone shown on this map represent some of the world's best-known gems. All are popular and highly prized, but some are far rarer than others.

PEARLS IN JAPAN
*The shallow coastal waters of the
Japanese islands offer ideal conditions
for farming pearl oysters. Pearls are
organic gems and therefore independent
of geological conditions.*

Russia

*former
Czechoslovakia*

Afghanistan

China   Japan

Egypt

Pakistan

Myanmar
(Burma)

India

Thailand

Zaire

Sri Lanka

East Africa

Madagascar

Australia

WORLD DISTRIBUTION

This map shows the main
localities for 12 key gems.
Each gem may of course
occur in other places, but
probably not in sufficient
quantities to make its extraction economical.
Some sites, although
historically important,
may now be worked out.

RUBIES IN MYANMAR
*The rich mineral deposits of Mogok
in Myanmar (Burma) have yielded
some of the world's finest rubies,
extracted by traditional methods.
Sapphires are also mined here.*

PHYSICAL PROPERTIES

THE PHYSICAL PROPERTIES of gemstones, their hardness, their specific gravity or density, and the way they break or "cleave," depend on chemical bonding and the atomic structure within the stone. For example, diamond is the hardest natural material known, and graphite is one of the softest, yet both are made of the same element, carbon. It is the way in which the carbon atoms are bonded together in diamond that gives it a greater hardness and resilience.

HARDNESS

One of the key qualities of a gemstone, hardness may be measured by how well a stone resists scratching. Every stone can be tested and classified using the Mohs scale of hardness (below), which gives every mineral a figure from one to ten. Intervals between numbers on the scale are not equal, most obviously between nine and ten (see the Knoop scale, right). Hardness testing is destructive, however, and should be used on a gemstone only if other tests fail.

TESTERS
Each of these testing pencils is tipped with a Mohs mineral.

KNOOP SCALE
This scale shows the indentation caused by a diamond point when it meets the surface of a mineral. The 10 stages correspond to Mohs' points.

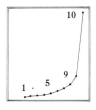

MOHS SCALE OF HARDNESS
The Mohs scale was devised by the German mineralogist Friedrich Mohs as a means of classifying the relative hardness of minerals. He took 10 common minerals and put them in order of "scratchability": each one will scratch those below it on the scale but will be scratched by those above it.

MOHS' MINERALS

1	2	3	4	5	6	7	8	9	10
TALC	GYPSUM	CALCITE	FLUORITE	APATITE	ORTHOCLASE	QUARTZ	TOPAZ	CORUNDUM	DIAMOND

SPECIFIC GRAVITY
The specific gravity (SG) of a gem is an indication of its density. It is calculated by comparing the stone's weight with the weight of an equal volume of water. The greater a stone's specific gravity, the heavier it will feel. For example, a small cube of pyrite (SG 5.2) will feel heavier than a larger piece of fluorite with an SG of 3.18; and a ruby (SG 4.00) will feel heavier than an emerald (SG 2.71) of similar size.

PYRITE

FLUORITE

RELATIVE WEIGHTS
The smaller piece of pyrite (SG 5.2) feels heavier than the fluorite (SG 3.18), because it is more dense.

CLEAVAGE AND FRACTURE

Gemstones may break in two ways: they either cleave or they fracture. Which way they break depends on the internal atomic structure of the stone. Gems that cleave tend to break along planes of weak atomic bonding (cleavage planes). These planes are usually parallel, perpendicular, or diagonal to the crystal faces (as both planes and faces are directly related to the stone's atomic structure). A gemstone may have one or more directions of cleavage, which may be defined as perfect (almost perfectly smooth), distinct, or indistinct (examples are shown right). Gems with perfect cleavage include diamond, fluorite, spodumene, topaz, and calcite.

When a gemstone breaks along a surface that is *not* related to its internal atomic structure, it is said to fracture. Fracture surfaces are generally uneven, and each type has its own descriptive name, shown in the examples below and right.

BARITE

ALBITE

◁ **PERFECT CLEAVAGE**
Fragile barite has three directions of easy cleavage, giving smooth surfaces.

△ **DISTINCT CLEAVAGE**
Although not perfectly smooth, albite's cleavage surfaces can be clearly seen.

◁ **INDISTINCT CLEAVAGE**
Cleavage direction is indistinct in aquamarine.

AQUAMARINE

DUMORTIERITE

△ **UNEVEN FRACTURE**
An uneven fracture surface is typical of fine-grained or massive gems like dumortierite.

OBSIDIAN

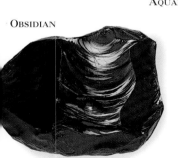

GOLD

NEPHRITE

△ **CONCHOIDAL FRACTURE**
The type most commonly found in gemstones, the name refers to the shell-like fracture surface.

HACKLY FRACTURE △
Rough, uneven fracture surface is seen on the right of this gold specimen.

SPLINTERY ▷ FRACTURE
Interlocking texture causes splintery fracture.

CRYSTAL SHAPES

Most MINERAL GEMSTONES are crystalline, with their atoms arranged in regular and symmetrical patterns, like a lattice; a few are amorphous, with no or only a weak crystal structure. Crystalline minerals may consist of a single crystal or of many in a group. Polycrystalline minerals are made up of many, usually small, crystals; in cryptocrystalline minerals, the crystals are too small to see without the aid of a microscope.

Crystalline minerals are made up of a number of flat surfaces called faces; the orientation of these faces defines the overall shape, which is known as the habit. Some minerals have a single, characteristic habit, such as pyramidal or prismatic; others may have several. A lump of crystalline mineral without a definite habit is called massive. Amorphous gemstones, like obsidian and tektites, have an irregular shape. Examples of common habits are shown right.

this natural glass cooled too fast for crystals to form

AMORPHOUS

some crystals form with a characteristic pyramidal end

PYRAMIDAL

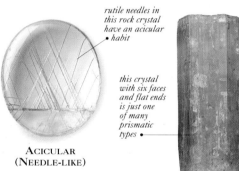

rutile needles in this rock crystal have an acicular habit

ACICULAR
(NEEDLE-LIKE)

this crystal with six faces and flat ends is just one of many prismatic types

PRISMATIC

TWINNING

Natural crystals are seldom perfect. Their growth is influenced by external factors such as temperature, pressure, space, and the medium in which they grow. One irregularity that may occur is known as twinning – when the internal structure of the crystal is repeated. Twins grow together in a number of different ways.

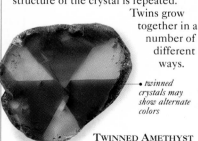

twinned crystals may show alternate colors

TWINNED AMETHYST

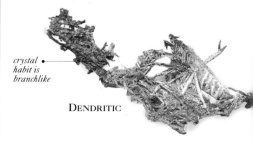

irregularly shaped mass with no apparent crystal habit

MASSIVE

crystal habit is branchlike

DENDRITIC

CRYSTAL SYSTEMS

Crystals are classified into seven different systems, according to the minimum symmetry of their faces. This depends on a crystal's axes of symmetry – imaginary lines (shown in black in the artworks on this page) around which a crystal may rotate and still show identical aspects. The number of times the same aspect may be seen – in one 360-degree rotation around an axis – defines that axis as twofold, threefold, etc., up to six.

PYRITE

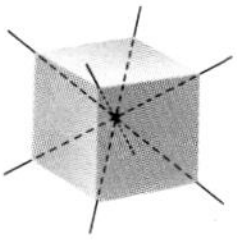

CUBIC
Crystals in the cubic system (also known as the isometric system) have the highest symmetry, e.g., cubes, octahedra, and pentagonal dodecahedra. The minimum symmetry is four threefold axes.

HEXAGONAL/ TRIGONAL
These systems (thought by some to be one system) share the same axis of symmetry. Hexagonal crystals have sixfold symmetry; trigonal crystals threefold.

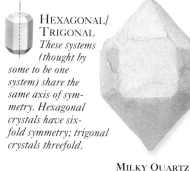

MILKY QUARTZ

TETRAGONAL
This system is defined by one fourfold axis. Typical crystal shapes include four-sided prisms and pyramids, trapezohedra, and eight-sided pyramids.

ZIRCON

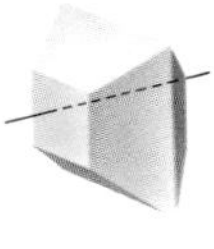

MONOCLINIC
The monoclinic system has a minimum symmetry of one twofold axis. Prisms with basal pinacoids are common crystal shapes found in this system.

TOPAZ

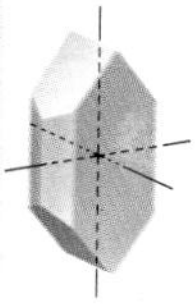

ORTHORHOMBIC
The minimum symmetry of this system is three twofold axes. Typical crystal shapes are rhombic prisms and pyramids with basal pinacoids, and rhombic double pyramids.

BRAZILIANITE

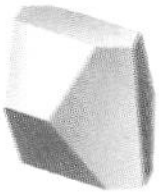

TRICLINIC
Triclinic crystals have no axis of symmetry, so gemstones within this system are the least symmetrical.

AXINITE

OPTICAL PROPERTIES

COLOR IS THE MOST OBVIOUS visual feature of a gem, but in fact it is just one of many optical properties, all of which are dependent upon light. The individual crystalline structure of a gemstone (see pp.18–19) interacts with light in a unique way and determines the optical properties of each gem species. Effects produced by light passing *through* a gem are described here; those produced by the *reflection* of light are described on pages 22–23.

WHAT MAKES COLOR?
The color of a gem depends largely on the way it absorbs light. White light is made up of the colors of the rainbow (spectral colors), and when it strikes a gem some spectral colors are "preferentially absorbed." Those that are not absorbed pass through or are reflected back, giving the gem its color. Each gem in fact has a unique color "fingerprint" (known as its absorption spectrum), but this is visible only when viewed with a spectroscope (see p.38). To the naked eye, many gems look the same color.

SPLITTING LIGHT THROUGH A PRISM
The splitting of white light into its spectral colors is called dispersion. It gives gems their internal fire.

ALLOCHROMATIC GEMS
Allochromatic ("other-colored") gems are colored by trace elements or other impurities that are not an essential part of their chemical composition. Corundum, for example, is colorless when pure, but impurities in it (usually a metal oxide) create the red stones we know as rubies, blue, green, and yellow sapphires, and orange-pink padparadscha. Allochromatic gems are often susceptible to color enhancement or change.

RUBY (RED CORUNDUM)

PURE CORUNDUM

SAPPHIRE (BLUE CORUNDUM)

IDIOCHROMATIC GEMS
The color of idiochromatic ("self-colored") gems comes from elements that are an essential part of their chemical composition. Thus idiochromatic gems generally have only one color or show only a narrow range of colors. Peridot, for example, is always green, because the color is derived from one of its essential constituents, iron.

PERIDOT

PERIDOT

MULTICOLORED GEMS

A crystal that consists of different-colored parts is called multicolored. It may be made up of two colors (bicolored), three (tricolored), or more. The color may be distributed unevenly within the crystal or in zones associated with growth. The many different varieties of tourmaline probably show the best examples of multicoloring, showing as many as 15 different colors or shades within a single crystal.

bicolored crystals can make attractive gemstones; junctions of color zones may be distinct (as here) or gradual

WATERMELON TOURMALINE

PLEOCHROIC GEMS

Gems that appear one color from one direction but that exhibit one or more other shades or colors if viewed from different directions are known as pleochroic. Amorphous or cubic stones show one color only; tetragonal, hexagonal, or trigonal stones show two colors (dichroic); orthorhombic, monoclinic, or triclinic stones may show three colors (trichroic).

iolite is strongly pleochroic: colorless from one direction, blue when rotated 90 degrees

IOLITE (BLUE ASPECT)

IOLITE (COLORLESS ASPECT)

REFRACTIVE INDEX (RI)

When a ray of light meets the surface of a polished gemstone, some light is reflected but most passes in. Because the gem has a different optical density from that of air, the light slows down and is bent from its original path (refracted). The amount of refraction within a gem is called its refractive index (RI) and, with the DR (below), can be used to help identify the stone.

calcite is highly birefractive, producing double images

CALCITE

SEEING DOUBLE
Zircon's back facets look doubled, due to strong double refraction (DR).

BIREFRACTION (DR)
When viewed through a refractometer (far right), cubic minerals like spinel are singly refractive, showing a single shadow edge; doubly refractive minerals like tourmaline split light rays in two, producing two shadow edges. The difference between the two gives the "birefraction" (DR).

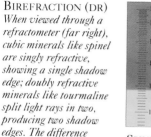

SPINEL

TOUR-MALINE

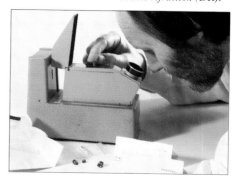

LUSTER

The overall appearance of a gemstone, its luster, is determined by the way light is reflected from its surface. This is related to the degree of surface polish, which increases with the stone's hardness. Gemologists use a variety of terms to describe luster and its degree of intensity. "Splendent" means that the stone reflects light like a mirror; but if little light is reflected, the luster may be described as "earthy" or "dull." Stones with a luster comparable to diamond are described as "adamantine" and are the most desirable. Most transparent, faceted gems have a glasslike, "vitreous" luster; the precious metals have a metallic luster; and organic gems show a range, from "resinous" to "pearly" and "waxy." Some gemstone species vary in their luster: garnets, for example, range from the resinous hessonite garnet to the adamantine luster of demantoid garnet. Rough lazulite and howlite have a dull, earthy luster, which is vitreous after polishing.

hematite crystals, like pyrite and the precious metals, • display metallic luster

METALLIC LUSTER

hard and highly polished, the look of a diamond defines • adamantine luster

the glasslike luster of this ruby is the most common • for cut stones

ADAMANTINE LUSTER

VITREOUS LUSTER

waxy luster is most commonly associated with • turquoise

the greasy luster of this polished imperial jadeite is comparatively rare

WAXY LUSTER

GREASY LUSTER

organic • gems, like this amber bead, may occur in a range of lusters, depending on the nature of the material

satin spar gypsum is commonly cited to describe silky luster •

RESINOUS LUSTER

SILKY LUSTER

INTERFERENCE

Interference is an optical property caused by the reflection of light off structures within a gemstone. This internal reflection gives a play of color. In some stones it will produce the full range of the spectral colors; in others just one color may predominate. In opal, interference occurs because of the structure of the stone itself – spheres arranged in regular three-dimensional patterns. This produces the rainbow effect called iridescence, shown by a number of other gems such as hematite, labradorite, and iris quartz.

In moonstone feldspar, interference at the junctions of its internal layers (thin, alternating layers of different types of feldspar) produces a shimmering effect just below the surface of the stone, known as adularescence, opalescence, or a schiller (sheen).

moonstone feldspar exhibits a bluish white shimmer or sheen

ADULARESCENCE

light reflected from labradorite gives a rainbow effect

IRIDESCENCE

LIGHT LAYERS
Iridescence appears at layers within labradorite.

hematite shows a play of color

IRIDESCENCE

blue and green may predominate within opal

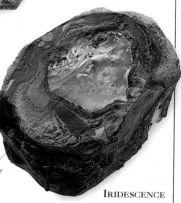

IRIDESCENCE

CAT'S-EYES AND STARS

When a gemstone is cut *en cabochon* (with a domed, polished surface), light reflecting from the stone's internal features, such as cavities or fibrous or needlelike inclusions (see pp.24–25), may create a cat's-eye effect (chatoyancy) or star stones (asterism). One set of parallel fibers gives rise to the cat's-eye effect; two sets of fibers produce a four-rayed star, three sets of fibers a six-rayed star, and so on.

reflection from acicular (needle-like) rutile crystals gives a six-rayed star

parallel fibers within the stone produce the cat's-eye "flash"

SAPPHIRE STAR STONE

CHRYSOBERYL CAT'S-EYE

NATURAL INCLUSIONS

INCLUSIONS ARE INTERNAL features of gems. They may be solids, liquids, or gases that the crystal enclosed as it grew, or cleavages, cracks, and fractures that filled (or partly filled) after the host material finished growing. Although usually regarded as flaws, inclusions today are often seen as adding interest to a stone. They can also be invaluable in identifying a gem, because some are peculiar to a particular species, while others occur only in a particular locality.

FORMATION OF INCLUSIONS

Solid inclusions have usually formed before the host stone – the crystals of the host have grown around them and enclosed them. They may be distinct crystals or amorphous masses. Solids and liquid inclusions formed at the same time as the host are aligned to its atomic structure. For instance, the stars in star rubies and sapphires are caused by needlelike crystals of rutile, which formed parallel to the crystal faces at the same time as the host corundum crystals. Cavities filled or fractures healed after the formation of the host give inclusions that resemble feathers, insect wings, or fingerprints.

MICROSCOPE
A microscope that magnifies between 10 and 40 times is one of the most useful instruments for examing inclusions in gemstones.

• *stone holder to allow viewing from any angle*

DIAMOND WITH GARNET
Solid inclusions may be the same gem type as the host or different – like the garnet in this diamond.

PERIDOT "WATER LILY" (MAGNIFIED 30 TIMES)
Inclusions that look like water lily leaves are a typical feature of peridot from Arizona. Each inclusion consists of a central chromite crystal surrounded by liquid droplets.

MOONSTONE "CENTIPEDES"
These insectlike inclusions (magnified 35 times) are a common feature of moonstone. In fact they are parallel cracks caused by strain.

INSECT IN AMBER
Insects are sometimes found trapped in amber, caught by the sticky resin as it was exuded. To create a natural effect, insects are sometimes added to imitation amber.

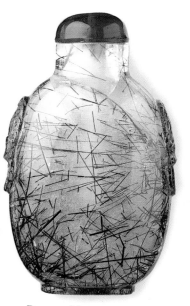

RUTILE NEEDLES
This carved rock crystal perfume bottle contains inclusions of needlelike rutile crystals. Tourmaline and gold are also found in rock crystal.

ALMANDINE GARNET (ABOVE)
Magnified 45 times, the gray patch on the left is a rounded apatite inclusion. The bright interference colors to the right are due to a zircon crystal.

EMERALD (LEFT)
Rectangular cavities with tails (magnified 40 times) are sometimes found in natural Indian emeralds.

FACETING

THE MOST USUAL METHOD of fashioning a gem is to cut the surface into a number of flat faces, known as facets. This gives the stone its final shape, or cut. The gem cutter, or lapidary, tries to show the stone's best features, taking into account its color, clarity, and weight. The lapidary may have to compromise to retain its weight and therefore value. The blue diagrams on the opposite page, which show the most popular cuts, are used throughout the book.

HOW A STONE IS FACETED

There are several stages in the cutting of a gemstone, each of which may be carried out by a different expert. In our example, a rough diamond crystal is fashioned into a brilliant cut. This is the most popular cut for this stone because it maximizes the gem's naturally strong light dispersion. However, because each stone is a different shape, or has imperfections within it, or because retaining the weight is of paramount importance, the cut in its ideal form (the "make") may not be possible. Nevertheless, the essential aim is to make the diamond bright and sparkling, showing flashes of color called fire. To this end, the size, number, and angles of the facets are mathematically calculated. The rough crystal is sawn or cleaved to obtain a basic workable piece, then turned on a lathe against another diamond to give it a round shape. The facets are then cut and polished in stages, and the stone is given a final polish before mounting.

1. ROUGH
A rough diamond crystal is selected for faceting.

crown •

bezel •

2. CUT
The top is cut off, and the stone rounded on a lathe by another diamond.

• girdle

3. GRIND
The central facet – the flat table – is ground first, then the bezel facets.

table
• facet

4. TOP AND BOTTOM
More facets are put on in groups and in sequence: the star facets and upper girdle facets on the crown; then the lower girdle facets and the culet on the pavilion (the underside).

• bezel facet

upper girdle facet •

• star facet

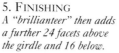

5. FINISHING
A "brillianteer" then adds a further 24 facets above the girdle and 16 below.

6. MOUNTING
After a final polish, the stone is mounted in precious metal.

BRILLIANT CUTS

The brilliant cut is the most popular for diamonds and for many other stones, particularly colorless ones. It ensures that maximum light is reflected out through the front, giving brightness and fire. Variations in the outline give the oval, the pear-shaped pendeloque, and the boat-shaped marquise or navette.

BRILLIANT-CUT SAPPHIRE

ROUND   **OVAL**

RINGS OF FIRE
These gold rings from the house of Cartier are set with diamonds, sapphires, rubies, and emeralds, in a variety of cuts from brilliant to fancy.

STEP CUTS

The step cut (or trap cut) shows colored stones to advantage, having a rectangular or square table facet and girdle, with parallel rectangular facets. The corners of fragile gems may be removed, making octagonal stones – as, for example, in most emeralds.

OCTAGONAL STEP-CUT SPESSARTINE

TABLE   **SQUARE**   **OCTAGON**

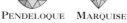

BAGUETTE   **OVAL**

MIXED CUTS

Mixed-cut stones are usually rounded in outline, with the crowns (above the girdle) cut as brilliants and the pavilions (below the girdle) step cut. Sapphires, rubies, and most transparent colored stones are cut in this style.

CUSHION

MIXED

MIXED-CUT PERIDOT

FANCY CUTS

These have several possible outlines, such as triangular, kite-shaped, lozenge-shaped, pentagonal, or hexagonal. The cut may be used for rare gems, or to make the most of a flawed or irregularly shaped gem.

FANCY-CUT HELIODORE

PENDELOQUE   **MARQUISE**   **SCISSORS**

POLISHING, CARVING, AND ENGRAVING

PRECIOUS METALS AND GEMS – usually massive, microcrystalline stones and organics – can be worked by polishing, carving, or engraving. Polishing is the oldest form of fashioning. Carving produces three-dimensional objects by cutting them from a larger mass of material. Engraved images are made by scratching out lines or holes or by cutting away to leave a raised image. Carving and engraving require tools harder than the material being worked.

POLISHING

The shine given to the surface of a stone – by rubbing it either with grit or powder or against another stone – is its polish. Dark-colored gemstones and those that are translucent or opaque, for instance opal and turquoise, are often polished rather than faceted, as are organic gems. They may be polished as beads or as flat pieces to be used in inlay work, or cut *en cabochon* with a smooth, rounded surface and usually a highly polished, domed top and flat base.

drum contains abrasive grits and polishing powders

PEBBLE POLISHER
Gem fragments of similar hardness may be turned into attractive pebbles (left) by tumbling in a drum containing abrasive grits and polishing powders (right).

MOTOR-DRIVEN TUMBLING DRUM FOR POLISHING

CARVING

Carving usually refers to the cutting of decorative objects from a larger mass. Stones as hard as 7 on the Mohs scale were carved in ancient Egypt, Babylonia, and China. Impure corundum (emery) was used for carving and engraving in India; nowadays a hand-held chisel or turning machine is used. Popular stones for carving include serpentine, Blue John, malachite, azurite, rhodonite, and rhodochrosite.

CHINESE CARVING

Carving of gemstones in China dates back to the Neolithic period. The most prized material was imported nephrite jade, and decorative objects like this model pagoda are still made.

ENGRAVING

Engraving usually refers to the decoration of the surface of a gemstone by the excavation (scratching out) of lines, holes, or trenches with a sharp instrument, known as a graver or turin. Cameos and intaglios are perhaps the most popular of all engraved objects. A cameo is a design (often a human profile) in flat relief, around which the background has been cut away. In an intaglio it is the subject, not the background, that is cut away, creating a negative image that may be used as a seal in clay or wax. Intaglios were particularly popular with the ancient Greeks and Romans and are still prized by collectors.

GOLD ENGRAVING

The surface of gold and other precious metals used in jewelry may be decorated with intricate patterns, using a hand-held chisel called a graver.

Engraved gemstones gained prominence in Europe in the Renaissance period. During the Elizabethan period in Britain cameo portraits were often given as gifts, particularly among the nobility. All through the ages, layered stones have been used for cameos or intaglios, with onyx and sardonyx particularly popular. Other gems suitable for engraving include rock crystal, amethyst, citrine, beryl, peridot, garnet, lapis lazuli, and hematite, as well as organic materials such as ivory and jet.

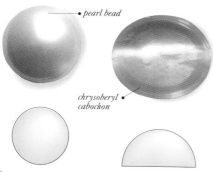

pearl bead

chrysoberyl cabochon

BEAD

Spherical gems such as pearls may be pierced and threaded as beads on necklaces.

CABOCHON

This simple cut is used to display colors and optical effects in opaque and translucent stones.

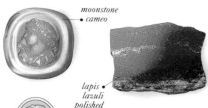

moonstone cameo

lapis lazuli polished slab

MODERN DESIGNS

This citrine prism, with its clean, architectural lines and exquisite engraving, demonstrates the flair and craftsmanship of modern designers. Its maker, Bernd Munsteiner, uses conventional cuts to create classic modern jewels akin to pieces of sculpture. Bernd Munsteiner is one of many artists working in Idar-Oberstein in Germany. Together with Hong Kong, Idar-Oberstein is considered to be one of the most important centers for carving and engraving gemstones today.

CARVING

The cameo symbol used in this book denotes both carvings and engravings.

POLISHED STONE

Decorative stones given a flat, polished surface may be used in ornaments and jewelry.

ENGRAVED CITRINE

GEMS THROUGH THE AGES

MANKIND'S FASCINATION with gemstones is as old as history itself. People everywhere, throughout the ages, have followed a natural instinct to collect things of beauty and value, and have used whatever gemstones they found locally – from shells to sapphires – to adorn themselves. Today, there are more gem-producing areas than ever before, new stones are increasingly available, and jewelry designs continue to evolve. But the inherent attraction of gems – their beauty, durability, and rarity – remains the same.

FIRST USES

Gem materials were probably first used as much for their durability as their beauty. But beauty was not ignored, even then. For example, the Stone Age obsidian ax below has been wrought to be attractive as well as practical, and ancient civilizations did fashion gems purely for adornment. Although most were primitive in design, some were highly intricate, with painted surfaces. Down the ages, gems have also been offered as prestigious gifts, and their portability and intrinsic value gave them a natural use as currency.

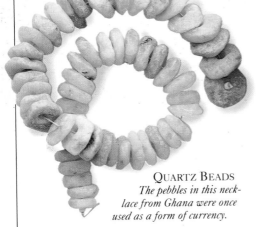

QUARTZ BEADS
The pebbles in this neck-lace from Ghana were once used as a form of currency.

EARLY COLLECTORS

The earliest collectors found gems with no more equipment than a stick or shovel, a basket, and a sharp eye. Similar Stone Age tools found in the Mogok area of Myanmar show that rubies have been mined there for thousands of years – and the same methods of panning the stream with wicker baskets are used today. Evidence of more organized early mining – for example, abandoned mines and waste dumps – is found in the Urals of Russia, on the shores of the Mediterranean, in Cornwall, England, and in many other places worldwide.

OBSIDIAN AX
A natural volcanic glass, obsidian could be fashioned into a razor-sharp tool or weapon.

EMERALD IN LIMESTONE
Emerald has been sought after for many thousands of years. The earliest known mines date back to Egypt, 2000 BC.

ANCIENT JEWELRY

Little jewelry made before the 18th century survives. The best examples are probably those of ancient Egypt. Many of these pieces are gold set with gems such as turquoise, lapis lazuli, and carnelian. It shows the great skill of the Egyptian goldsmiths: the gold refined, annealed, and soldered; the gems fashioned – probably using silica sand, a technique also known to the ancient Chinese. The Romans went on to develop the polished stone rather than the setting. The art of the goldsmith and lapidary survived in the Dark Ages, though in medieval times gothic style was functional – mainly buckles, clasps, and rings.

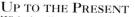

MERMAN
In this typical 16th-century pendant, a pearl forms the torso, with diamonds and rubies set in gold around it.

CLOTHED IN JEWELS
Civilizations through the ages have used jewelry for adornment. This late 18th-century miniature shows an Indian woman clothed in richly jeweled necklaces, earrings, bracelets, and amulets.

UP TO THE PRESENT

With the discovery of the Americas in the 15th century, European trade in gemstones expanded, and 16th- and 17th-century jewelers could use gems from all over the world. With the rise of an affluent merchant class, jewelry became more widely owned and diamonds first became fashionable. In the 20th century, an increase in demand for affordable gems and the scarcity of the most valuable will doubtless continue the trend to use more varied gem species in jewelry.

GEM-ENCRUSTED MODERN BROOCH
Jewelry has passed through many styles, from baroque in the 16th century and floral themes in the 17th, to Art Deco and beyond in the 20th.

HISTORY AND FOLKLORE

THERE ARE NUMEROUS myths and legends associated with gems. Some tell of cursed stones; others of stones with special powers of healing, or that protect or give good luck to the wearer. Some of the largest known diamonds have legends associated with them that have been told and retold over centuries, and many now lost are surrounded by tales of intrigue and murder. Some mines are thought to be cursed – probably rumors spread by the mine owners to keep unwanted prospectors away. In Myanmar (Burma), for instance, where all gemstones belonged to the monarch, the belief that anyone who took a stone from a mine would be cursed may have been deliberately cultivated to curb losses of a valuable national asset.

DEATH MASK
This Aztec funeral mask adorned with turquoise may have speeded entry to the next world.

PERUVIAN GOD
This 12th-century ceremonial knife from Peru is made from gold adorned with turquoise. The handle has been formed into the image of a deity.

CRYSTAL GAZING

Since Greek and Roman times, balls of polished rock crystal have been used to see into the future. The difficulty of finding a flawless piece large enough to be polished adds to the mystique. The mystic gazes at the ball, lets the eyes go out of focus, and then interprets the misty "image."

rock crystal ball supported by Japanese dragons

THUMB GUARD
This 17th-century ring, mounted with rubies and emeralds, was designed to protect an archer's thumb when releasing arrows.

CRYSTAL BALL

BIRTHSTONES

Certain gems have traditionally been associated with different months of the year and are thought lucky or important for people born under their influence. This probably stems from the ancient belief that gems came from the heavens. Many cultures associate gems with the signs of the zodiac, and others associate them with the months of the year. The selection varies from country to country, perhaps influenced by availability of gems, local traditions, or fashions. The custom of wearing birthstone jewelry started in 18th-century Poland and has since spread throughout the world. The most popular selection is shown at right.

JANUARY (GARNET)

FEBRUARY (AMETHYST)

MARCH (AQUAMARINE)

APRIL (DIAMOND)

MAY (EMERALD)

JUNE (PEARL)

JULY (RUBY)

AUGUST (PERIDOT)

SEPTEMBER (SAPPHIRE)

OCTOBER (OPAL)

NOVEMBER (TOPAZ)

DECEMBER (TURQUOISE)

SIGNS OF THE ZODIAC
This rock crystal is shaped with 12 pentagonal faces, each engraved with one of the signs of the zodiac.

CRYSTAL HEALING

Belief in the healing properties of gems has a very long history, as the rituals of medicine men in ancient tribes attest. Crystal healers today believe that each gem has the power to influence the health and well-being of a specific part of the body. The light reflected off stones placed on vital nerve points is thought to be absorbed by the body, supplying it with healing energy.

ROCK CRYSTAL
Prized for their beauty and clarity, rock crystals are often chosen for use in crystal healing.

CRYSTAL PENDANT
Gems worn close to the skin are believed to heal or protect.

SYNTHETIC GEMSTONES

SYNTHETIC GEMSTONES are made in laboratories or factories, not in rocks. They have virtually the same chemical composition and crystal structure as natural gemstones, so their optical and physical properties are very similar.

However, they can usually be identified by their distinctive inclusions. Many gems have been synthesized in the laboratory but only a few are produced commercially. These are generally used for industrial and scientific purposes.

MAKING A SYNTHETIC

Man has tried to replicate gemstones for thousands of years, but it was not until the late 1800s that any substantial success was achieved. In 1877, French chemist Edmond Frémy grew the first gem-quality crystals of reasonable size (see bottom right), and then around 1900 August Verneuil devised his technique to manufacture ruby. With a few modifications, the Verneuil flame-fusion method is still in use today. The powdered ingredients are dropped into a furnace and melt as they fall through a flame hotter than 3,630°F (2,000°C), fusing into liquid drops. These drip on to a pedestal and crystallize. As the pedestal is withdrawn, a long, cylindrical crystal, which is known as a boule, forms.

FLUX-MELT TECHNIQUE
Pioneered by the French chemist Edmond Frémy, the flux-melt technique is still used to make emeralds. The powdered ingredients are melted and fused in a solvent (flux) in a crucible. The material must be kept at a very high temperature for months, before being left to cool very slowly.

FLUX-MELT SYNTHETIC EMERALD

FLAME-FUSION CORUNDUM
Synthetic corundum manufactured by flame-fusion grows as a single mass called a boule. It has the same inner structure as a natural crystal and can be cut to shape.

synthetic ruby crystals grown in a crucible •

corundum boules tend to split down their length •

EDMOND FRÉMY
French chemist Edmond Frémy, the first to grow emerald crystals of a reasonable size, went on to grow ruby crystals by melting aluminum oxide and chromium in a crucible.

• pedestal on which boule forms

CORUNDUM BOULES

SHAPES AND COLORS

Because of the way they are made, synthetic gems may show subtle differences in shape and color that help distinguish them from their natural counterparts. For instance, corundum produced by flame fusion has curved growth lines rather than straight ones, because the ingredients have not mixed together fully. Some synthetic gems may also suffer from uneven color distribution. Flame-fusion spinel is manufactured to imitate gems such as ruby, sapphire, aquamarine, blue zircon, tourmaline, peridot, and chrysoberyl.

SYNTHETIC SPINEL
Synthetic spinel (above), colored red, may make a better imitation gem than flame-fusion ruby (left).

DISTINCTIVE INCLUSIONS

Synthetic gems have different inclusions from those of natural gems, so often the best way to tell them apart is to examine them with a loupe (below) or a microscope. Synthetic inclusions may be typical of a process, or of a synthetic gem species. For instance, in Verneuil rubies, gas bubbles have well-defined outlines; in flux-melt emeralds (right), characteristic veil and feather patterns form.

GILSON FLUX-MELT EMERALD

GILSON EMERALD INCLUSIONS
Synthetic emeralds from the French manu-facturer Gilson have characteristic veil-like inclusions. The gems are made from poor-quality material by a flux-melt method.

LOUPE
This hand-held lens is powerful enough to assist in gem identification. With its ten-fold magnification it may be possible to distinguish between natural and synthetic inclusions.

GILSON LAPIS LAZULI

GILSON TURQUOISE

GILSON GEMS

Lapis lazuli, turquoise, and coral produced by the French manufacturer Gilson are similar to their natural counterparts but are not true synthetics because their optical and physical properties differ from the natural gems. Gilson lapis lazuli, for example, is more porous and has a lower specific gravity.

GILSON CORAL

IMITATION AND ENHANCEMENT

IMITATION GEMS have the appearance of their natural counterparts, but their physical properties are different. They are intended to deceive. Manmade materials, such as glass and synthetic spinel, have been used to imitate many different gems, but natural stones can also be modified to resemble more valuable gems. It is possible to enhance authentic gemstones by hiding cracks and flaws, or by using heat treatment or irradiation to improve their color.

GLASS IMITATIONS

Glass has been used for centuries to imitate gemstones. It can be made either transparent or opaque in almost any color, and, like many gems, it has a vitreous luster. At first sight, therefore, it may easily be mistaken for the real thing. However, it can usually be detected by its warmer feel and by the evidence of wear and tear that results from its greater softness. Chipped facets and internal swirls and bubbles are common. In addition, unlike most of the gems it imitates, glass is singly refractive.

GLASS "RUBY"

glass imitations often contain pronounced inclusions

• glass can be made to imitate almost any transparent gem

SNOWFLAKE INCLUSION IN GLASS

OPAL IMITATIONS

Gemologists call the flashes of color in opal its "play of color," or iridescence. It is caused by the interference of light from the minute spheres of silica gel that make up the gem. This structure is imitated to great effect in opals made by the French manufacturer Gilson, although the difference can be seen in the mosaiclike margins of the patches of color (see p.135). There are various other opal imitations, including stones made of polystyrene latex, or of different pieces assembled as one. In an opal doublet (two pieces) the top is natural precious opal, but the base is common (potch) opal, glass, or chalcedony. A triplet (three pieces) has an additional protective dome of rock crystal.

GILSON OPAL

POLYSTYRENE LATEX OPAL

SLOCUM STONES

American manufacturer John Slocum developed imitation opals with a good play of color, but they lack the silky, flat color patches of genuine opal and the structure looks crumpled when magnified.

GARNET-TOPPED DOUBLET

One of the most common composite stones (stones made of more than one piece) is the garnet-topped doublet, or GTD. A thin section of natural garnet is cemented to a colored glass base, which gives the GTD its apparent color. The deception is most easily seen at the junction of the two layers, which may be obvious.

red garnet crown

green glass base

GARNET-TOPPED DOUBLET

GTD JUNCTION
Changes in color and luster are visible where garnet and glass meet.

DIAMOND IMITATIONS

Many natural materials have been used to imitate diamond, but zircon is the most convincing. Synthetic imitations are popular, but each has its faults (right). Imitations can usually be detected by testing the heat conductivity of the stone.

heavy, lacks fire

YTTRIUM ALUMINUM GARNET (YAG)

CUBIC ZIRCONIA

heavier than diamond

softer, more fire

STRONTIUM TITANATE

HEAT TREATMENT

Heating may enhance or change the color or clarity of some gems. Techniques range from throwing gems in a fire to "cook," to the use of sophisticated equipment. The outcome is certain for some gems (like aquamarine, which changes from green to blue), but less so for others.

BROWN ZIRCON HEATED TO BLUE

IRRADIATION

Gems may change color if exposed to radiation. This may come from radioactive elements within the Earth's crust or from artificial sources. Natural radiation may take millions of years to have an effect, while artificial irradiation may take only a few hours to change a gem's color. In some cases a gem will later revert to its original color or may fade with time. Many changes can be reversed or modified by heat treatment.

IRRADIATED, HEAT-TREATED TOPAZ

STAINING

Stains, dyes, or chemicals can alter the appearance of a gem, coating just the surface or changing the whole specimen. For staining to be effective, a stone must be porous or contain cracks and flaws through which the color can enter. Porous white howlite, for example, can be stained to imitate turquoise.

STAINED HOWLITE

OILING

Oils may enhance a gem's color and disguise fissures and blemishes. It is common to oil emeralds in order to fill their natural cracks and flaws.

OILED EMERALD

COLOR KEY

WHEN IDENTIFYING a gemstone, a gemologist will hold it, feel it, and examine it from all angles. This is done to assess the appearance of the stone by noting the color, the luster, and any other features. A hand-held loupe (see p.35) may be used to search for scratches and flaws on the surface that may give an indication of hardness, while a search inside the stone may reveal characteristic inclusions. These features may be unique to one gem, but further tests may be necessary to identify synthetic or imitation stones. From this initial examination, however, the gemologist should know which tests to perform.

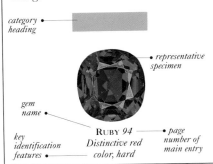

HOW THE COLOR KEY WORKS

This key puts all gems into one of seven color categories, though color varieties within some species may appear (or be listed, if not pictured in the book itself) in more than one. Each color category is divided into three sections: gems that are always that color, gems usually that color, and gems sometimes that color.

category heading

representative specimen

gem name

key identification features

RUBY *94*
Distinctive red color, hard

page number of main entry

RUBY

ALMANDINE GARNET

RED GLASS

SPECTROSCOPE
Many gems appear the same color, but can be distinguished when viewed with a spectroscope (above). This reveals an absorption spectrum (left) that is unique to each gemstone (see p.21).

COLORLESS GEMSTONES

ALWAYS COLORLESS

HAMBERGITE *115*
Perfect cleavage, large birefraction

PHENAKITE *98*
Silvery look if well cut

ALBITE *130*
Vitreous to pearly luster

GOSHENITE *77*
Spiky inclusions common

BERYLLONITE *118*
Lacks fire, soft, brittle

ROCK CRYSTAL *81*
Vitreous luster,
transparent

PETALITE *129*
Vitreous luster,
transparent

DATOLITE *129*
Tinge of yellow,
green, or white

ACHROITE *102*
Extremely
rare

USUALLY COLORLESS

SCHEELITE *70*
Very soft, good
fire, uncommon

CELESTINE *105*
Soft, cut for
collectors only

DIAMOND *54*
Adamantine
luster, good fire

DANBURITE *110*
Yellow/pink tinge,
bright, lacks fire

CERUSSITE *105*
Adamantine luster,
high density, soft

SOMETIMES COLORLESS

DOLOMITE *99*
Soft, vitreous
to pearly luster

EUCLASE *129*
Rare, black
mineral inclusions

MOONSTONE *123*
Opalescence, blue
or white sheen

COLORLESS
ORTHOCLASE *122*
Three good cleavages

SCAPOLITE *71*
Rare, vitreous
luster

FLUORITE *66*
Soft, lacks fire,
hematite inclusions

ZIRCON *72*
Adamantine
luster, good fire

SAPPHIRE *96*
Rare, high density,
extremely hard

APATITE *79*
Fairly soft

OTHER GEMS
ENSTATITE *111*
GROSSULAR *61*
TOPAZ *106*

RED OR PINK

ALWAYS RED OR PINK

ROSE QUARTZ *83*
Cloudy, distinctive pinkish color

KUNZITE *120*
Strongly pleochroic, good cleavage

MORGANITE *78*
Distinctive color, hard

THULITE *116*
Distinctive color mix, massive

PINK GROSSULAR *60*
Distinctive color, fine-grained, opaque

TUGTUPITE *74*
Opaque, may be mottled, massive

RHODOCHROSITE *100*
Fine-grained, banded; also clear faceted stones

RHODONITE *132*
Black veins in massive material

RED BERYL *78*
Extremely rare, seldom cut

RUBY *94*
Distinctive red color, hard

ALMANDINE *59*
Distinctive color, high luster

PYROPE *58*
Distinctive color, inclusions rare

RUBELLITE *101*
Pleochroic, cat's-eye cabochons

USUALLY RED OR PINK

TAAFFEITE *80*
Extremely rare, fairly hard

SPESSARTINE *58*
Lacelike inclusions, rare at gem quality

SOMETIMES RED OR PINK

JADEITE *124*
Dimpled surface when polished

TOPAZ *106*
Distinctive color, hard, high density

WATERMELON TOURMALINE *103*
Distinctive colors

SAPPHIRE *97*
High density, hard, pleochroic

CORAL *142*
*Grain on surface,
soft, may fade*

SPINEL *64*
*Hard, singly
refractive*

JASPER *92*
*Distinctive
color, opaque*

OTHER GEMS
ZIRCON *73*
RUTILE *71*
SMITHSONITE *99*
SCAPOLITE *71*
GARNET-TOPPED
DOUBLET *61*

WHITE OR SILVER

ALWAYS WHITE OR SILVER

MILKY QUARTZ *85*
*Distinctive milky
white color*

PLATINUM *52*
*Metallic luster, high
density, opaque*

SILVER *50*
*Metallic luster,
soft, opaque*

HOWLITE *128*
*Very soft,
chalky, opaque*

IVORY *146*
*Soft, growth
lines on surface*

MEERSCHAUM *119*
*Chalky, opaque,
fine-grained, soft*

GYPSUM *128*
*Silky to vitreous
luster, soft*

USUALLY WHITE OR SILVER

PEARL *138*
*Pearly luster,
very soft*

SHELL *144*
*Iridescent,
very soft*

SOMETIMES WHITE OR SILVER

CALCITE *98*
*Soft, large
birefraction*

SERPENTINE *127*
*Vitreous to greasy
luster, translucent*

NEPHRITE *125*
*Tough interlocking
structure*

OTHER GEMS
AGATE *88*
CORAL *142*
OPAL *134*
MOONSTONE *123*

YELLOW TO BROWN GEMSTONES

ALWAYS YELLOW–BROWN

ANGLESITE *114*
*High density,
fragile, good fire*

CITRINE *83*
*Distinctive
color*

BRAZILIANITE *118*
*Fragile, brittle,
fairly soft, rare*

SINHALITE *114*
*Pleochroic, large
birefraction*

HELIODOR *77*
*Pleochroic, hard,
pastel shades*

GOLD *48*
*Distinctive
color, soft*

PADPARADSCHA *95*
*Distinctive orange-
pink color, hard*

CARNELIAN *93*
*Translucent,
reddish brown*

FIRE OPAL *134*
*Low density,
transparent*

SARDONYX *90*
*Distinctive white
bands*

HESSONITE *60*
*Granular
inclusions*

SUNSTONE *130*
*Bright metallic
inclusions*

HYPERSTHENE *112*
*Reddish iridescence,
fairly soft*

DRAVITE *102*
*Pleochroic, showing two
shades of body color*

CASSITERITE *70*
*High density,
good fire*

TORTOISESHELL *144*
*Distinctive mottling
on surface*

SMOKY QUARTZ *84*
*Distinctive grayish
brown color*

EPIDOTE *121*
*Strongly pleochroic,
fragile, rarely cut*

OTHER GEMS
TOPAZOLITE *107*
PYRITE *63*

USUALLY YELLOW–BROWN

AMBLYGONITE *132*
*Vitreous to pearly
luster*

**YELLOW
ORTHOCLASE** *122*
Fragile, cat's-eyes

VESUVIANITE *74*
*Pleochroic, vitreous
to adamantine luster*

SPHALERITE *63*
*Good fire, metallic
to vitreous luster*

TITANITE *121*
*Very good fire,
pleochroic*

AMBER *148*
*Very soft,
resinous luster*

**AVENTURINE
QUARTZ** *85*
Platy inclusions

AXINITE *133*
*Pleochroic,
easily chipped*

ENSTATITE *111*
*Fragile, distinctive
absorption spectrum*

STAUROLITE *117*
*Opaque, twinned
crystals cross-shaped*

SOMETIMES YELLOW–BROWN

RUTILE *71*
*Good fire, needle-
like inclusions*

PREHNITE *115*
*Usually cloudy
and translucent*

SCHEELITE *70*
*Fairly soft,
good fire*

**CHATOYANT
QUARTZ** *86*
Fibrous structure

MOSS AGATE *89*
*Translucent,
mosslike pattern*

ARAGONITE *104*
*Very soft, micro-
crystalline*

SPESSARTINE *58*
*Hard, lacelike
inclusions*

BARITE *104*
*High density,
very soft*

CHRYSOBERYL *108*
*Hard, strongly
pleochroic*

OTHER GEMS

DIAMOND *54*
DEMANTOID *62*
FLUORITE *66*
ZIRCON *72*
APATITE *79*
SAPPHIRE *96*
TOURMALINE *101*
TOPAZ *106*
KORNERUPINE *113*

GREEN GEMSTONES

ALWAYS GREEN

CHRYSOCOLLA *126*
*Distinctive color,
opaque, very soft*

EMERALD *75*
*Distinctive color,
seldom flawless*

PERIDOT *113*
*Distinctive oily
green color*

HIDDENITE *120*
*Distinctive color,
pleochroic*

DIOPTASE *99*
*Distinctive color,
large birefraction*

BLOODSTONE *93*
*Opaque, red
spots*

UVAROVITE *59*
*Distinctive color,
crystals fragile*

PRASE *92*
*Translucent, dark
green color*

MALACHITE *126*
*Characteristic bands
of color, soft*

MOLDAVITE *137*
*Glassy, inclusions of
bubbles and swirls*

ALEXANDRITE *108*
*Color changes,
pleochroic, high density*

ANDALUSITE *110*
*Very strong
pleochroism*

USUALLY GREEN

SERPENTINE *127*
*Vitreous to greasy
luster, fairly soft*

JADEITE *124*
*Fine-grained,
may be dimpled*

DIOPSIDE *119*
Large birefraction

DEMANTOID *62*
*Asbestos inclusions,
adamantine luster*

AVENTURINE QUARTZ *85*
Platy inclusions,
vitreous luster

NEPHRITE *125*
Tough interlocking structure,
greasy to pearly luster

OTHER GEMS
PREHNITE *115*

SOMETIMES GREEN

MICROCLINE *123*
Distinctive blue-
green color

AGATE *88*
Translucent,
distinct banding

WATERMELON
TOURMALINE *103*
Bicolored

DIAMOND *56*
Hardest natural
substance, good fire

SAPPHIRE *96*
High density,
hard, pleochroic

APATITE *79*
Distinctive
absorption spectrum

ZIRCON *72*
Good fire, adaman-
tine to resinous luster

GROSSULAR
GARNET *61*
Vitreous luster

GARNET-TOPPED
DOUBLET *61*
Two parts joined

ENSTATITE *111*
Distinctive
absorption spectrum

KORNERUPINE *113*
Strongly pleochroic,
rare as gem quality

SPHALERITE *63*
Very soft, good
fire, high density

OTHER GEMS
FLUORITE *66*
KYANITE *133*
TOURMALINE *103*
SMITHSONITE *99*
EUCLASE *129*

BLUE OR VIOLET GEMSTONES

ALWAYS BLUE OR VIOLET

AQUAMARINE *76*
Tubular inclusions,
pleochroic

LAZULITE *128*
Often
mottled

HAUYNE *68*
Small stones,
rarely cut

TURQUOISE *131*
Distinctive color,
fragile

INDICOLITE *101*
Strongly
pleochroic

AZURITE *126*
Distinctive color,
fragile, soft

LAPIS LAZULI *69*
Distinctive blue,
pyrite inclusions

SODALITE *68*
Distinctive
blue color

ZOISITE *116*
Strongly
pleochroic

AMETHYST *82*
Tigerstripe
inclusions

USUALLY BLUE OR VIOLET

SILLIMANITE *111*
Distinctly pleochroic,
good cleavage

DUMORTIERITE *117*
Usually massive,
distinctive color

BENITOITE *80*
Good fire,
birefraction

IOLITE *112*
Strongly
pleochroic

KYANITE *133*
Pleochroic,
brittle, flaky

SOMETIMES BLUE OR VIOLET

FLUORITE *66*
Lacks fire, soft,
good cleavages

TOPAZ *106*
Pleochroic, hard,
tearlike inclusions

ZIRCON *72*
Good fire, adaman-
tine to resinous luster

SMITHSONITE *99*
Distinctive
blue color

SAPPHIRE *95*
High density,
hard, pleochroic

SCAPOLITE *71*
*Cat's-eyes, fibrous
inclusions*

SPINEL *64*
*Hard, singly
refractive*

AXINITE *133*
*Pleochroic,
brittle*

OTHER GEMS
APATITE *79*
AGATE (STAINED) *88*
HOWLITE (STAINED) *128*
DIAMOND *54*
EUCLASE *129*
CHRYSOBERYL *108*
GARNET-TOPPED
DOUBLET *61*

BLACK GEMSTONES

ALWAYS BLACK

HEMATITE *100*
*Metallic luster,
opaque, iridescent*

SCHORL *103*
*Opaque,
vitreous luster*

JET *140*
*Very soft, coal-like
smell when warm*

USUALLY BLACK

OBSIDIAN *136*
*Glassy, fairly hard,
bubblelike inclusions*

SOMETIMES BLACK

MELANITE *62*
*Adamantine to
vitreous luster*

DIAMOND *54*
*Adamantine
luster, hard*

TEKTITE *137*
*Glassy, cracks
on surface*

CORAL *142*
*Sensitive to
heat, soft*

IRIDESCENT GEMSTONES

OPAL *134*
*Iridescent colors,
may dry and crack*

FIRE AGATE *87*
*Iridescence resembles
oily rings of color*

LABRADORITE *130*
*Iridescence on dark
body color*

MOTHER-OF-PEARL *145*
*Blue and purple
iridescence on surface*

Crystal structure Cubic	Composition Gold	Hardness 2½

GOLD

The color of gold depends upon the amount and type of impurities it contains. Native gold is typically golden yellow, but in order to vary its color and increase its hardness for use in jewelry, gold may be alloyed with other metals. Silver, platinum, nickel, or zinc may be added to give a pale or white gold. Copper is added for rose or pink gold; iron for a tinge of blue. Gold purity is defined by the proportion of pure gold metal present, expressed as its carat (ct) value. The purity of gold used in jewelry varies from 9 carat (37½ percent or more pure gold), through 14, 18, and 22 carat, to 24 carat, which is pure gold. In many countries, gold jewelry is "hallmarked" to indicate its degree of purity.

• **OCCURRENCE** Gold is found in igneous rocks and in associated quartz veins, often in small quantities invisible to the naked eye. It is also concentrated in secondary "placer" deposits – as nuggets or grains in river sands and gravels. Gold may still be extracted from placer deposits by the traditional panning method, but modern commercial mining involves large earth-moving machinery and concentrated acids for processing the ore. The main gold-bearing rocks occur in Africa, California and Alaska, Canada, the former USSR, South America, and Australia.

• **REMARK** Gold has been used for coins, decoration, and jewelry for thousands of years. It is attractive and easily worked and wears well.

smooth, waterworn surface

GOLD NUGGET

metallic luster

octahedral crystals of gold in a skeletal framework

CRYSTALLIZED GOLD NUGGET

typically rounded and flattened grains

grains collected from placer deposits by panning

white quartz

gold usually occurs as fine grains, not groups of crystals like these

GOLD GRAINS

GOLD IN QUARTZ MATRIX

SG 19.30	RI None	DR None	Luster Metallic

crystalline nugget

TIE PIN
This unusual piece of jewelry features a gold nugget set into a gold tie pin.

GOLD, DIAMONDS, AND PEARLS
This gold neckpiece is set with pink pearls and clusters of diamonds. Gold is a popular setting for precious stones as it is easy to fashion and is hard-wearing and resistant to acids and tarnishing.

groups of diamonds

natural pearl

GOLD BANGLE
This flexible bracelet is made from 18-carat rose and yellow gold.

GOLD MOLD
This ivy leaf motif set was made by casting 18-carat gold in a wax mold.

hallmark

GOLD BANGLE
The hallmark that shows the purity of worked gold is just visible on this delicate bangle. In this case, it indicates the gold is 18 carat.

softness of gold accommodates intricate working

GOLD RING
Gold is a popular and resilient material for rings. Here it is the setting for a green demantoid garnet.

square-cut demantoid garnet

Crystal structure Cubic	Composition Silver		Hardness 2½

SILVER

Silver usually occurs in massive form as nuggets or grains, although it may also be found in wiry, dendritic (treelike) aggregates. When newly mined or recently polished, it has a characteristic bright, silver-white color and metallic luster. However, on exposure to oxygen in the air, a black layer of silver oxide readily forms, tarnishing the surface. Because of this, and the fact that it is too soft to be used in most jewelry in its pure or native form, silver is often alloyed with other metals or given a covering layer of gold. Electrum, an alloy of gold and silver in use since the time of the ancient Greeks, contains 20–25 percent silver. Sterling silver contains 92½ percent or more pure silver (and usually some copper), and Britannia silver has a silver content of 95 percent or more. Both alloys are used as standards to define silver content.

• OCCURRENCE Most silver is a by-product of lead mining and is often associated with copper. The main silver mining areas of the world are South America, the USA, Australia, and the former USSR. The greatest single producer of silver is probably Mexico, where silver has been mined for almost 500 years. The finest native silver, which occurs naturally in the shape of twisted wire, is from Kongsberg, Norway.

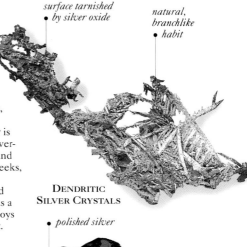

surface tarnished by silver oxide

natural, branchlike habit

DENDRITIC SILVER CRYSTALS

polished silver

patches of copper

POLISHED SLICE OF SILVER AND COPPER ORE

maker's mark

crystals have wirelike habit

SILVER WINE CUP
This part-gilt silver cup was fashioned in 1493, when silver was valued as highly as gold.

dendritic silver from Kongsberg is renowned for its quality

NATIVE SILVER FROM KONGSBERG, NORWAY

SG 10.50	RI None	DR None	Luster Metallic

rose
gold

TOWER BROOCHES
These modern silver
brooches, made by
British silversmith
V. Ambery-Smith,
have additional
decoration in rose
and yellow gold.

*highly
polished silver*

SILVER BRACELET
This sterling silver
bracelet also features
18-carat gold thread.

silver

*18-carat
gold thread*

yellow
gold

SILVER DISH
Fashioned in 1973, this
dish features a leaf
motif border made
from oxidized
silver.

*oxidation
alters color
of silver*

*ornate
carving*

WATCH CASE
Because of its softness,
silver is extremely
popular for fine
metalwork, as
seen in this
18th-century
watch.

*silver lends a
simple elegance
to modern
designs*

MODERN USES
Silver is prized for
ornamental items,
such as these key
rings. Today it is also
used in electronics
and photography.

Crystal structure Cubic	Composition Platinum	Hardness 4

PLATINUM

Platinum has been used for thousands of years, but it was not recognized as a chemical element until 1735. Of the three precious metals – gold, silver, and platinum – it is the rarest and the most valuable. Chemically inert and resistant to corrosion, platinum does not tarnish when exposed to the atmosphere, unlike silver. It is silvery gray, gray white, or white in color, opaque, and has a metallic luster. It is slightly more dense than pure gold and about twice as dense as silver. Early jewelers had difficulty achieving the 3,223°F (1,773°C) needed to melt platinum: it was not until the 1920s that the technology was developed sufficiently to work this precious metal.

• OCCURRENCE Platinum forms in igneous rocks, usually as ores in which the grains of platinum are often too minute to be seen with the naked eye. It may also occur in secondary "placer" deposits in river sands and gravels, and glacial deposits – usually as grains, more rarely as nuggets. The main occurrences of platinum have been in South Africa, Canada (Sudbury), the USA (Alaska), Russia (the River Perm and other rivers running down from the Urals), Australia, Colombia, and Peru.

• REMARK Although nuggets had been set in rings before 1920, most platinum jewelry dates from after this time. Soft and easy to carve, platinum is often fashioned into quite intricate designs.

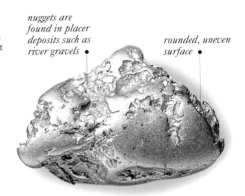

nuggets are found in placer deposits such as river gravels •

rounded, uneven surface •

PLATINUM NUGGET

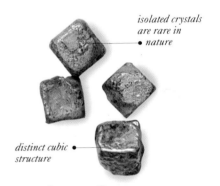

isolated crystals are rare in • nature

distinct cubic • structure

ISOLATED CRYSTALS

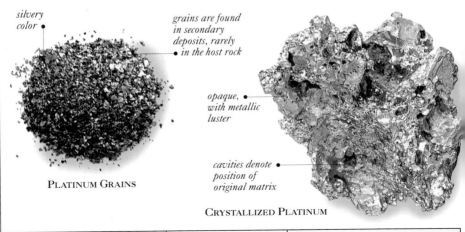

silvery color •

grains are found in secondary deposits, rarely • in the host rock

PLATINUM GRAINS

opaque, • with metallic luster

cavities denote • position of original matrix

CRYSTALLIZED PLATINUM

SG 21.40	RI None	DR None	Luster Metallic

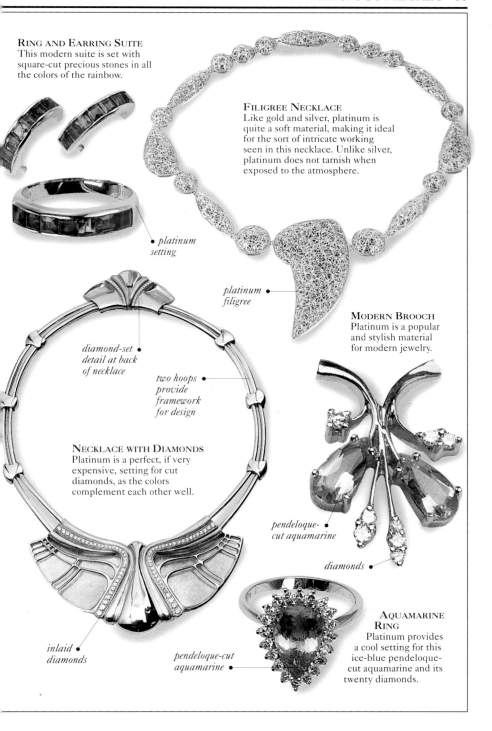

RING AND EARRING SUITE
This modern suite is set with square-cut precious stones in all the colors of the rainbow.

FILIGREE NECKLACE
Like gold and silver, platinum is quite a soft material, making it ideal for the sort of intricate working seen in this necklace. Unlike silver, platinum does not tarnish when exposed to the atmosphere.

• platinum setting

platinum • filigree

MODERN BROOCH
Platinum is a popular and stylish material for modern jewelry.

diamond-set • detail at back of necklace

two hoops • provide framework for design

NECKLACE WITH DIAMONDS
Platinum is a perfect, if very expensive, setting for cut diamonds, as the colors complement each other well.

pendeloque- • cut aquamarine

diamonds •

inlaid • diamonds

pendeloque-cut aquamarine •

AQUAMARINE RING
Platinum provides a cool setting for this ice-blue pendeloque-cut aquamarine and its twenty diamonds.

Crystal structure Cubic	Composition Carbon		Hardness 10

DIAMOND

Diamond is the hardest mineral on Earth, and this, combined with its exceptional luster and brilliant fire, has made it the most highly prized of all gems. Pure, colorless diamond is the most popular, but other varieties – from yellow and brown to green, blue, pink, red, gray, and black – are also found, depending on the impurities present. Because of the uniform arrangement of their constituent carbon atoms, diamond crystals are well formed – usually octahedral with rounded edges and slightly convex faces. Their perfect cleavage facilitates the early stages of fashioning (see p.26), but they can be polished only by other diamonds.

• OCCURRENCE Diamond forms at high temperatures and pressures 50 miles (80 km) or more underground. When India and later Brazil were the main producers, most diamond came from secondary sources, such as river gravels. However, since the discovery of diamond in kimberlite rock in South Africa (around 1870), its extraction has involved processing vast quantities of rock. Australia is the main producer today; other localities include Ghana, Sierra Leone, Zaire, Botswana, Namibia, the former USSR, the USA, and Brazil.

• REMARK Diamonds are graded by the four C's: color, cut, clarity, and carat (weight).

colored diamonds, such as this yellowish green variety, are known as "fancy"

BRILLIANT CUT

most diamonds are faceted as a brilliant cut, which brings out their natural fire

BRILLIANT CUT

pale pink stone

brilliant cut reflects as much light as possible out through front of stone

BRILLIANT CUT

subtle gray-green color

minimum light leakage through back facets

BRILLIANT CUT

pink-red variety

green and black inclusions

rounded edges

typical convex surfaces

FIVE UNPOLISHED DIAMOND CRYSTALS

diamonds may be transparent to opaque

adamantine luster

SG 3.52	RI 2.42	DR None	Luster Adamantine

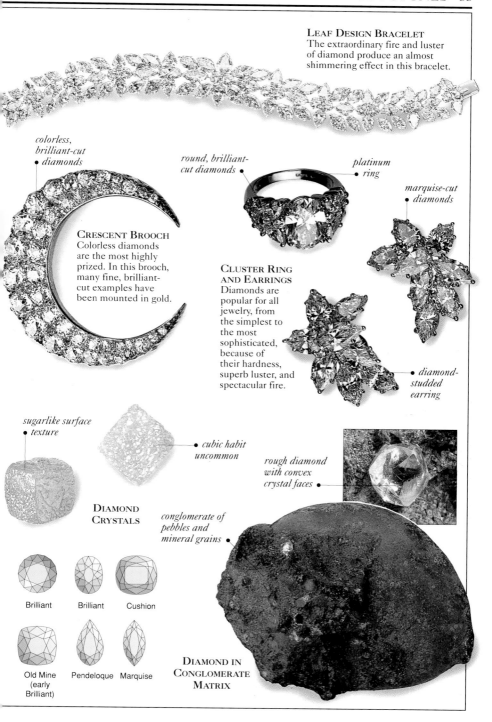

LEAF DESIGN BRACELET
The extraordinary fire and luster of diamond produce an almost shimmering effect in this bracelet.

colorless, brilliant-cut diamonds •

round, brilliant-cut diamonds •

platinum • ring

marquise-cut • diamonds

CRESCENT BROOCH
Colorless diamonds are the most highly prized. In this brooch, many fine, brilliant-cut examples have been mounted in gold.

CLUSTER RING AND EARRINGS
Diamonds are popular for all jewelry, from the simplest to the most sophisticated, because of their hardness, superb luster, and spectacular fire.

• diamond-studded earring

sugarlike surface • texture

• cubic habit uncommon

rough diamond with convex crystal faces •

DIAMOND CRYSTALS

conglomerate of pebbles and mineral grains •

Brilliant	Brilliant	Cushion

Old Mine (early Brilliant)	Pendeloque	Marquise

DIAMOND IN CONGLOMERATE MATRIX

Crystal structure Cubic	Composition Carbon		Hardness 10

different color varieties are caused by minute traces of other minerals

unusual, semitranslucent, milky white stone

opaque, black "bort" variety derives color from graphite inclusions

Inclusions in this diamond cause asterism in the form of a double six-rayed star.

BRILLIANT CUT

pinkish brown color

colorless stone marred by black, carbon-filled inclusions

BRILLIANT-CUT BORT DIAMOND

dodecahedral (12-sided) habit

BRILLIANT CUT

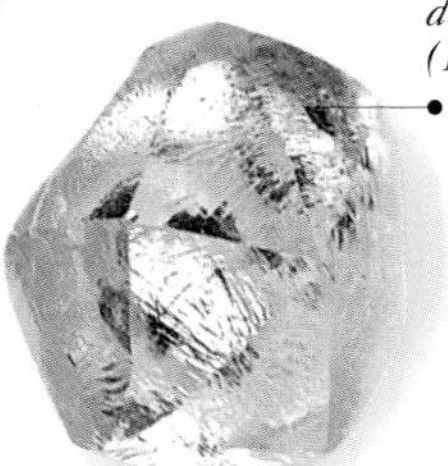

dark green color due to exposure to radioactive radium

DIAMOND CRYSTAL

colorless diamond crystal

volcanic, diamond-bearing kimberlite rock, first identified in Kimberley, South Africa

BRILLIANT CUT

characteristic three-sided face, known as a trigon

FANCY DIAMOND CRYSTAL

DIAMOND IN KIMBERLITE

SG 3.52	RI 2.42	DR None	Luster Adamantine

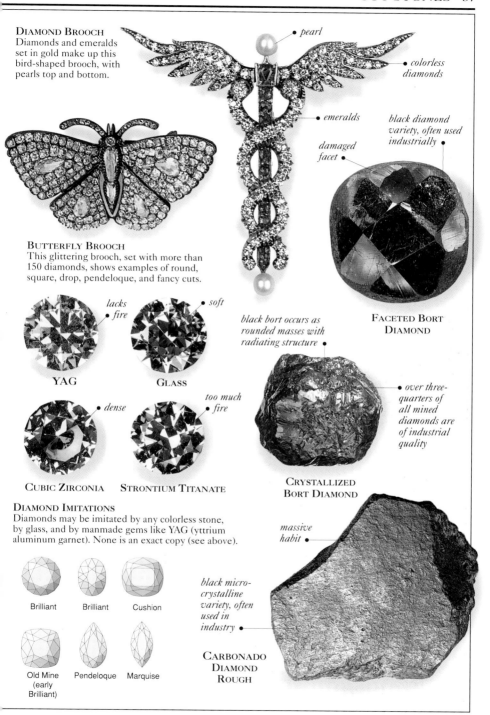

DIAMOND BROOCH
Diamonds and emeralds set in gold make up this bird-shaped brooch, with pearls top and bottom.

pearl

colorless diamonds

black diamond variety, often used industrially

emeralds

damaged facet

BUTTERFLY BROOCH
This glittering brooch, set with more than 150 diamonds, shows examples of round, square, drop, pendeloque, and fancy cuts.

lacks fire

soft

YAG

GLASS

black bort occurs as rounded masses with radiating structure

FACETED BORT DIAMOND

dense

too much fire

over three-quarters of all mined diamonds are of industrial quality

CUBIC ZIRCONIA

STRONTIUM TITANATE

CRYSTALLIZED BORT DIAMOND

DIAMOND IMITATIONS
Diamonds may be imitated by any colorless stone, by glass, and by manmade gems like YAG (yttrium aluminum garnet). None is an exact copy (see above).

massive habit

Brilliant

Brilliant

Cushion

black micro-crystalline variety, often used in industry

Old Mine (early Brilliant)

Pendeloque

Marquise

CARBONADO DIAMOND ROUGH

Crystal structure Cubic	Composition Magnesium aluminum silicate	Hardness 7¼

PYROPE (GARNET)

The blood red color of pyrope is due to its iron and chromium content. It rarely has inclusions, but when present they are rounded crystals or have irregular outlines. As with all garnets, pyrope has no cleavage, and fracture is subconchoidal to uneven.
• **OCCURRENCE** Pyrope is found in volcanic rock and alluvial deposits and may, along with certain other minerals, indicate the presence of diamond-bearing rocks. Localities include the USA (Arizona), South Africa, Argentina, Australia, Brazil, Myanmar, Scotland, Switzerland, and Tanzania.
• **REMARK** Pyrope comes from the Greek *pyropos*, meaning fiery. Swiss and South African pyropes are lighter red than stones from Bohemia, where pyrope jewelry has been made for over 500 years.

brilliant-cut crown

vitreous luster

OVAL BRILLIANT CUT

BOHEMIAN EARRINGS
Perfectly transparent, clear, uniformly colored crystals like these were popular for jewelry in the 18th and 19th centuries.

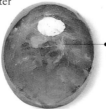

fiery red Bohemian pyrope

hornblende schist matrix

pyrope crystals

PYROPE CRYSTALS IN MATRIX

Brilliant   Mixed

SG 3.80	RI 1.72–1.76	DR None	Luster Vitreous

Crystal structure Cubic	Composition Manganese aluminum silicate	Hardness 7

SPESSARTINE (GARNET)

Gem-quality spessartine is uncommon. It is bright orange when pure, but an increase in the iron content makes the stone darker orange to red. Inclusions are lace- or featherlike.
• **OCCURRENCE** Spessartine occurs in granitic pegmatites and alluvial deposits. It is found in Sri Lanka, Madagascar, Brazil, Sweden, Australia, Myanmar, and the USA; also Germany and Italy, but crystals there are too small to facet.
• **REMARK** Spessartine is named after the Spessart district of Bavaria, Germany. It can be confused with hessonite garnet or yellow topaz, but on close examination of inclusions it is distinguishable.

liquid inclusions

vitreous luster

OCTAGONAL STEP CUT

lacy inclusions

flat crystal face

Brilliant   Step   Cabochon

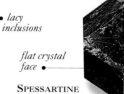

CABOCHON

SPESSARTINE CRYSTAL

SG 4.16	RI 1.79–1.81	DR None	Luster Vitreous

Crystal structure Cubic	Composition Iron aluminum silicate	Hardness 7½

ALMANDINE (GARNET)

Almandine is generally darker red than pyrope and may appear black, although pinkish red specimens are found. It is usually opaque or subtranslucent, but the rare transparent stones have high luster. Although dense, almandine is brittle, and facet edges chip. Many stones show characteristic inclusions, and four-rayed stars may be seen when the stones are cut *en cabochon*. The darker almandines are frequently cut as cabochons or used as abrasives in garnet paper. The underside of dark almandine is often hollowed out to let more light filter through the stone.

• **OCCURRENCE** Almandine is found in metamorphic rocks, such as garnet mica schist, and less frequently in granitic pegmatites. It has a worldwide occurrence.

• **REMARK** Slices of garnet have been used in windows in churches and temples, and legend has it that Noah suspended garnet in the ark in order to disperse light. Garnet was once said to cure melancholy and to warm the heart.

• *brilliant cut enhances fiery red color*

ROUND BRILLIANT CUT

Needlelike crystals of rutile or hornblende are typical inclusions in almandine.

hollow back allows in more light

black mineral inclusions •

CABOCHON

DROP EARRINGS
The pale pinkish red almandine garnets of these 18th-century earrings have been faceted in the rose cut and set in gold.

Cabochon

Mixed

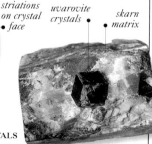
rounded almandine crystals •

granulite matrix •

cut shows triangular faces

ALMANDINE CRYSTALS IN MATRIX

SG 4.00	RI 1.76–1.83	DR None	Luster Vitreous

Crystal structure Cubic	Composition Calcium chromium silicate	Hardness 7½

UVAROVITE (GARNET)

The attractive bright green color of uvarovite is due to the presence of chromium. The crystals are very fragile, with subconchoidal to uneven fracture.

• **OCCURRENCE** Uvarovite occurs in serpentine rocks. The best clear crystals are found in the Urals in Russia, lining cavities or rock fissures. Other sources are Finland, Turkey, and Italy.

striations on crystal face •

uvarovite crystals •

skarn matrix

UVAROVITE CRYSTAL

Brilliant

UVAROVITE CRYSTALS IN MATRIX

SG 3.77	RI 1.86–1.87	DR None	Luster Vitreous

Crystal structure Cubic	Composition Calcium aluminum silicate	Hardness 7¼

HESSONITE (GROSSULAR GARNET)

cinnamon-colored stone

OVAL MIXED CUT

Grossular garnets occur in a very wide range of colors, from colorless to black. Their name is derived from the first specimen ever found, a distinctive gooseberry green color (see opposite). The orange-brown color of hessonite grossular garnet is due to manganese and iron inclusions.

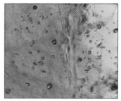

Hessonite garnet has swirls of inclusions, giving it a honeylike appearance.

• OCCURRENCE The best hessonite garnets are found in Sri Lanka in metamorphic rocks or gem gravels and sands. In Madagascar, hessonite is often referred to as cinnamon stone. Other localities include Brazil, Canada, and Siberia (Russia), as well as the USA (Maine, California, and New Hampshire).

• REMARK Both the ancient Greeks and Romans made cameos, intaglios, and cabochons from hessonite, and faceted stones for jewelry.

granular inclusions

hessonite has no cleavage

color due to manganese and iron

OVAL MIXED CUT

twinned crystals

bright orange-brown hessonite crystals

Brilliant   Mixed

ROUND MIXED CUT

HESSONITE CRYSTALS ON MATRIX

SG 3.65	RI 1.73–1.75	DR None	Luster Vitreous to resinous

Crystal structure Cubic	Composition Calcium aluminum silicate	Hardness 7

PINK GROSSULAR (GARNET)

Pure grossular garnet is colorless, but impurities incorporated during its formation cause a wide range of colors. This pink variety results from the presence of iron.

• OCCURRENCE Pink grossular is found in Mexico, usually as a massive form in metamorphic rocks. Crystals are rare. It also occurs in South Africa.

• REMARK Pinkish grossular from Mexico may be known as rosolite.

limestone matrix

pink grossular crystals

CRYSTALS IN MATRIX

Polished

GROSSULAR GARNET POLISHED SLAB

pink and green banded material may be called Transvaal jade

SG 3.49	RI 1.69–1.73	DR None	Luster Vitreous

Crystal structure Cubic	Composition Calcium aluminum silicate	Hardness 7

GREEN GROSSULAR (GARNET)

There are two varieties of green grossular: one is found as transparent crystals, the other is massive. Massive green grossular from South Africa is called Transvaal jade, after its main source and because it resembles jade. It may contain black specks of the mineral magnetite. Since the 1960s, a transparent green grossular garnet, tsavorite, has been mined in Kenya. Massive green grossular is used as a decorative stone; tsavorite is faceted as a gem.

- **OCCURRENCE** Found in Canada, Sri Lanka, Pakistan, the former USSR, Tanzania, South Africa, and the USA. Kenya is the main source for tsavorite.
- **REMARK** The name "grossular" is derived from the botanical name of the gooseberry, *R. grossularia*. Massive grossular garnet of a gooseberry green color was first discovered in the former USSR. Since then it has also been found in Hungary and Italy.

chromium and vanadium create • rich green color

BRILLIANT CUT

BEAD NECKLACE Polished massive green grossular beads have a speckly appearance due to magnetite inclusions.

distinctive gooseberry • color

MASSIVE POLISHED SLAB

groups of green grossular crystals •

GREEN GROSSULAR CRYSTALS IN MATRIX

Brilliant   Bead   Polished

SG 3.49	RI 1.69–1.73	DR None	Luster Vitreous

Crystal structure Variable	Composition Variable	Hardness Variable

GARNET-TOPPED DOUBLET

A doublet is a stone made of two separate pieces cemented together to create the appearance of a precious stone. Glass topped by red almandine garnet is the most common form, with green glass used to imitate emerald, blue to imitate sapphire. Once joined, the stone is faceted and polished.

- **REMARK** These stones were very popular in Britain and the rest of Europe in the Victorian era.

red almandine garnet cemented to • green glass base

luster and color change at junction of stones •

CUSHION-CUT DOUBLET

ALMANDINE GARNET ON GLASS BASE

Brilliant   Brilliant

SG Variable	RI Variable	DR None	Luster Variable

Crystal structure Cubic	Composition Calcium iron silicate	Hardness 6½

ANDRADITE GARNET

Garnets containing titanium and manganese are grouped as andradite garnet. The most valuable is demantoid, whose emerald green color is due to the presence of chromium. It has a higher dispersion than diamond and can be recognized by the characteristic "horsetails," which are fine, hairlike inclusions of asbestos. Topazolite, the yellow variety of andradite garnet, varies from pale to dark yellow. Only small crystals are found. Melanite is generally a black form, but can also be dark red.

• OCCURRENCE The best demantoid is found in the Urals in Russia and is associated with gold-bearing sands and metamorphic rocks. Other localities include northern Italy, Zaire, and Kenya. Topazolite crystals are found in the Swiss and Italian Alps in metamorphic rocks. Melanite is found in metamorphic rocks and volcanic lavas; fine crystals are found on the island of Elba (Italy) and in France and Germany.

high fire gives flashes of • color

BRILLIANT-CUT DEMANTOID

Demantoid garnet has inclusions of fine, hair-like asbestos fibers, known as "horsetails."

"horsetail" • inclusions

typically worn facet edges due to softness of demantoid •

MIXED-CUT DEMANTOID

crystal face has vitreous to • metallic luster

BRILLIANT-CUT DEMANTOID

serpentine • matrix

demantoid crystals

DEMANTOID GARNET CRYSTALS IN MATRIX

MELANITE CRYSTAL

typically black, • opaque stone

BRILLIANT-CUT MELANITE

serpentine rock •

yellowish green crust of topazolite crystals •

TOPAZOLITE CRYSTALS IN MATRIX

 Brilliant

 Brilliant

 Mixed

SG 3.85	RI 1.85–1.89	DR None	Luster Vitreous to adamantine

Crystal structure Cubic	Composition Iron sulfide	Hardness 6

PYRITE

With its brassy yellow color, pyrite is often mistaken for gold (hence its other name, fool's gold). It occurs as cubes or as "pyritohedra," which have twelve faces, each with five edges. Pyrite has been used in jewelry for thousands of years, and examples from the ancient civilizations of the Greeks, Romans, and Incas have been found. Today it is used mainly in costume jewelry, but is brittle and requires careful cutting.
• OCCURRENCE Pyrite is found worldwide in igneous, metamorphic, and sedimentary rocks. Fine specimens come from Spain, Mexico, Peru, Italy, and France.
• REMARK The name comes from the Greek word *pyr*, meaning fire, since sparks are caused if pyrite is struck with a hammer.

• *striations may occur on crystal faces*

• *"pyritohedral" crystal has twelve faces*

PYRITE CRYSTAL

cubic form has six square faces •

Cabochon

Polished

PYRITE CRYSTAL

SG 4.90	RI None	DR None	Luster Metallic

Crystal structure Cubic	Composition Zinc sulfide	Hardness 3½

SPHALERITE

Sphalerite, also known as blende, is an important ore of zinc. It is usually very dark brown to black in color, but occasionally transparent, yellowish brown, or green stones are found that can be faceted. Since sphalerite is soft and has perfect cleavage, it is not suitable for jewelry, and is faceted for museums and collectors only.
• OCCURRENCE Sphalerite crystals are usually pseudo-octahedral in shape, forming in hydrothermal veins with other minerals, such as galena, quartz, pyrite, and calcite. Transparent, cuttable stones are found in Santander (Spain) and Mexico.
• REMARK In the past, sphalerite has often been confused with galena (lead sulfide), to which it is very similar.

back facets are doubled •

OCTAGONAL STEP CUT

rich reddish brown crystals •

worn facet edges •

high fire shows rainbow colors •

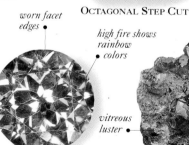

vitreous luster •

BRILLIANT CUT

Brilliant

Brilliant

Mixed

SPHALERITE
CRYSTALS IN MATRIX

SG 4.09	RI 2.36–2.37	DR None	Luster Metallic to vitreous

Crystal structure Cubic	Composition Magnesium aluminum oxide	Hardness 8

SPINEL

Spinel is found in a wide range of colors due to the presence of various impurities and is transparent to almost opaque. Red spinel colored by chromium and iron is the most popular, although for many years it was thought to be a variety of ruby. The orange-yellow or orange-red variety is called rubicelle (a diminutive of the French word for ruby). Blue spinel is colored by iron and less commonly by cobalt. Occasionally, inclusions of crystals such as magnetite or apatite may occur, and some Sri Lankan spinels may include zircon crystals surrounded by brown haloes. Star stones are rare, but when cut *en cabochon* may show 4-rayed or 6-rayed stars.

• **OCCURRENCE** Spinel occurs in granites and metamorphic rocks and is often found in association with corundum. Octahedral crystals and waterworn pebbles in a wide range of colors are found in the gem gravels of Myanmar, Sri Lanka, and Madagascar. Other localities include Afghanistan, Pakistan, Brazil, Australia, Sweden, Italy, Turkey, the former USSR, and the USA.

• **REMARK** Synthetic spinel has been manufactured since 1910. It has been used to imitate diamond or colored to imitate stones such as aquamarine and zircon. Blue synthetic spinel, colored by cobalt, has been used to imitate sapphire. The name may derive from the Latin word *spina*, meaning "little thorn," referring to the sharp points on some crystals.

vitreous luster

red stones originally known as Balas rubies

OCTAGONAL MIXED CUT

blood red stones sometimes known as ruby spinel

step cuts clearly visible

OVAL BRILLIANT CUT

pink stone from Myanmar

OCTAGONAL STEP CUT

bright red color

waterworn fragments found in gem gravels of Sri Lanka

CRYSTALS AND FRAGMENTS

red color due to chromium and iron impurities

AGGREGATE OF SPINEL CRYSTALS

SG 3.60	RI 1.71–1.73	DR None	Luster Vitreous

6-rayed star
brought out by
• cabochon cut

asterism is
rare in spinel

STAR-STONE CABOCHON

brilliant-cut
• crown facets

step-cut
• pavilion
facets

CUSHION MIXED CUT

pinkish mauve
color •

• liquid-filled
inclusions

CUSHION MIXED CUT

pale pinkish
purple stone from
Sri Lanka •

OCTAGONAL STEP CUT

blue
gahnospinel
contains zinc •

gahnospinel is
named after
Swedish chemist
• J.G. Gahn

MIXED-CUT GAHNOSPINEL

pale pinkish
• mauve color

• synthetics have
been manufactured
since 1910

**BRILLIANT-CUT
SYNTHETIC SPINEL**

dark, zinc-rich
• spinel crystals

Brilliant

Brilliant

Cushion

Step

Cabochon

Mixed

quartz matrix •

**SPINEL CRYSTALS
IN MATRIX**

Crystal structure Cubic	Composition Calcium fluoride	Hardness 4

FLUORITE

Formerly called fluorspar, fluorite has limited use as a gemstone because it is relatively soft and therefore easily scratched. However, the wide range of colors (including yellow, blue, pink, purple, and green), the frequent incidence of more than one color in a single specimen, and zoning or patchy distribution of color make it an interesting stone. Despite its fragility and perfect octahedral cleavage, stones are faceted (usually for collectors) and can be polished very brightly. Cabochons of fluorite have been capped with rock crystal (see p.81) to protect them from scratches.

• **OCCURRENCE** Localities include Canada, the USA (where some of the largest crystals are found), South Africa, Thailand, Peru, Mexico, China, Poland, Hungary, Czechoslovakia, Norway, England, and Germany. Pink octahedral crystals are found in Switzerland. A purple- and yellow-banded variety called Blue John occurs in England.

• **REMARK** The ancient Egyptians used fluorite in statues and to carve scarabs, and the Chinese have used it in carvings for more than 300 years. In the 18th century, fluorite was powdered in water to relieve the symptoms of kidney disease.

bright golden
• yellow color

• stones are
faceted for
collectors only

OCTAGONAL STEP CUT

iron ore
matrix

golden yellow
cubic fluorite
crystals •

**FLUORITE CRYSTALS
IN MATRIX**

fluorite is
soft and
difficult
• to facet

pale bluish
green color

OCTAGONAL STEP CUT

twinned
crystals •

green cubic
• crystals

**FLUORITE CRYSTALS
IN MATRIX**

black hematite
• inclusions

fluorite may be
mistaken for
glass, feldspar,
beryl, or quartz •

colorless
cubic
crystals •

CUSHION FANCY CUT

**FLUORITE
CRYSTALS IN MATRIX**

SG 3.18	RI 1.43	DR None	Luster Vitreous

pale pink
color

specks of black
hematite

CUSHION STEP CUT

tiny white
quartz crystals

cubic fluorite
crystals

**FLUORITE CRYSTALS
IN MATRIX**

cut stones may be
highly polished
and bright

mauve cubic
fluorite
crystals

white quartz
crystals

OCTAGONAL STEP CUT

**FLUORITE CRYSTALS
INTERGROWN WITH QUARTZ**

yellow and
purple
banding

smooth cleavage
surface

massive
habit

purple and
yellow
banding

green and
purple
banding

**CLEAVED FLUORITE
CRYSTAL**

FLUORITE ROUGH

BLUE JOHN VASE
This attractive banded
variety of fluorite has been
carved since Roman times.
The ancient Romans
believed that drinking
alcohol from a cup made
of Blue John would allow
the drinker to imbibe
without becoming drunk.

Cushion   Step   Mixed   Cameo

Crystal structure Cubic	Composition Sodium aluminum silicate	Hardness 5½

SODALITE

Sodalite, whose name reflects its sodium content, is found in all shades of blue and is a major constituent of the rock lapis lazuli (opposite), so the two are easily confused. However, unlike lapis lazuli, sodalite very rarely contains brassy pyrite specks, and it has a lower specific gravity. Sodalite may contain white streaks of the mineral calcite, and can be carved for use in jewelry.

• **OCCURRENCE** Sodalite is usually found as masses in igneous rocks. Crystals are very rare, but twelve-sided crystals have been found in the lavas of the volcano Vesuvius in Italy, although they are too small to be used in jewelry. Other localities include Brazil, Canada, India, Namibia, and the USA.

• **REMARK** The most important commercial source of sodalite is Bancroft in Ontario, Canada. It was discovered during a royal visit by Princess Margaret of England. For this reason, sodalite from Bancroft is sometimes called Princess Blue.

white calcite patches

vitreous luster

CABOCHON

semitranslucent stone

OVAL BRILLIANT CUT

white patches of calcite

veins of calcite

uneven fracture

Cabochon   Cameo

POLISHED
SODALITE

SODALITE ROUGH

SG 2.27	RI 1.48 (mean)	DR None	Luster Vitreous to greasy

Crystal structure Cubic	Composition Complex silicate	Hardness 6

HAUYNE

Hauyne forms part of lapis lazuli (opposite). It is usually intergrown with other minerals and is seldom found as individual crystals. Hauyne has perfect cleavage, making cutting difficult, so it is faceted primarily for collectors.

• **OCCURRENCE** Hauyne is found as small, rounded grains in volcanic rocks. Ancient volcanoes of Germany and Morocco are the best known sources.

faceted stones are typically small

BRILLIANT CUT

patches of crystals form in matrix

lilac hauyne crystals

matrix

Brilliant

HAUYNE
CRYSTALS
IN MATRIX

SG 2.40	RI 1.50 (mean)	DR None	Luster Vitreous to greasy

Crystal structure Various	Composition Rock containing lazurite and other minerals	Hardness 5½

LAPIS LAZULI (LAZURITE)

Lapis lazuli is a blue rock made up of several different minerals, including lazurite, sodalite, hauyne, calcite, and pyrite. The composition and color of lapis lazuli varies, but it is the intense dark blue, with minor patches of white calcite and brassy yellow pyrite, that is considered to be the best quality.
• **OCCURRENCE** Lapis lazuli is usually found as boulders or within limestones. The best quality lapis lazuli is from Afghanistan and has been used in many famous pieces, including the mask of Tutankhamen. Argentinian lapis lazuli is also of a high quality. A pale blue variety occurs in the former USSR and in Chile. Lapis lazuli from the USA is a darker shade of blue; Canadian specimens are lighter blue.
• **REMARK** Lapis lazuli has been worn in the belief that it will protect the wearer from evil. It has been imitated by stained jasper and by paste with inclusions of copper. Imitation lapis lazuli produced by Pierre Gilson in France has a composition very similar to natural lapis lazuli.

BEAD NECKLACE
Specks of pyrite and streaks of calcite are visible in these lapis lazuli beads.

pale patches of calcite

brassy pyrite

BUDDHA CARVING
This carving is made from the highest quality lapis lazuli from Afghanistan.

main ingredient of imitation stone is lazurite

brassy pyrite specks

imitation stone softer than natural lapis lazuli

GILSON IMITATION CABOCHON

GILSON IMITATION SLAB

veins of brassy pyrite

uneven fracture

blue color due to presence of lazurite

rock is sawn open and ground with grits to give flat surface

streaks of calcite

POLISHED LAPIS LAZULI SLAB

uneven fracture

LAPIS LAZULI ROUGH

Cabochon	Cameo	Polished

SG 2.80	RI 1.50 (mean)	DR None	Luster Vitreous to greasy

Crystal structure Tetragonal	Composition Calcium tungstate	Hardness 5

SCHEELITE

Scheelite is quite soft and is therefore faceted only for collectors of the unusual. It has high dispersion and good fire, and varies in color from a pale yellowish white to brown. Colorless synthetic scheelite is used to imitate diamond but can be distinguished by its birefraction. It may also be colored by trace metals in order to imitate other gemstones.
• OCCURRENCE Scheelite is found in pegmatites and metamorphic rocks. Very large crystals over 1 lb (0.5 kg) have been collected in Brazil, but generally, larger crystals are not sufficiently transparent to be faceted. Other localities include Australia, Italy, Switzerland, Sri Lanka, Finland, France, and England.

good fire •
scratches show stone is soft and easily damaged

corners cut off to avoid chipping

BRILLIANT CUT

creamy yellow scheelite crystals •

gray magnetite matrix •

SQUARE STEP CUT

SCHEELITE CRYSTALS IN MATRIX

Brilliant   Step   Mixed

SG 6.10	RI 1.92–1.93	DR 0.017	Luster Vitreous to adamantine

Crystal structure Tetragonal	Composition Tin oxide	Hardness 6½

CASSITERITE

Cassiterite is the principal ore of tin. It is usually recovered from mines as black opaque grains, which are of little use in jewelry. Crystals are generally short, stubby prisms, though transparent, reddish brown crystals with adamantine luster are sometimes found, and faceted for collectors. They could be confused with diamond, brown zircon, and titanite, but casserite has higher specific gravity and distinct dichroism.
• OCCURRENCE Cassiterite occurs in pegmatites and can be washed into alluvial deposits. Localities include the Malay Peninsula, England, Germany, Australia, Bolivia, Mexico, and Namibia.
• REMARK The name "cassiterite" comes from the Greek word, *kassiteros*, meaning tin.

double images of rear facets visible

colorless stone with yellowish tinge •

rare transparent, reddish brown stone

OVAL BRILLIANT CUT

black mineral • inclusions

opaque, short, prismatic • crystals

ROUND BRILLIANT CUT

CASSITERITE CRYSTALS IN MATRIX

Brilliant   Mixed

SG 6.95	RI 2.00–2.10	DR 0.100	Luster Adamantine

| Crystal structure Tetragonal | Composition Complex silicate | Hardness 6 |

SCAPOLITE

Also called wernerite after the German geologist A.G. Werner, scapolite ranges in color from pink, purple, blue, yellow, and gray to colorless. These colors reflect variations in composition, from sodium-rich to calcium-rich. Crystals are found as prisms that resemble sticks, giving rise to the name "scapolite," derived from the Greek words *scapos*, meaning rod, and *lithos*, meaning stone.
• **OCCURRENCE** Scapolite is found as crystals in pegmatites and in metamorphic rocks like mica schist and gneiss. It also occurs in massive form. Localities include Brazil, Myanmar, Canada, Kenya, and Madagascar.
• **REMARK** A cat's-eye effect can be seen in some pink and purple stones. Scapolite may easily be confused with amblygonite, chrysoberyl, and golden beryl.

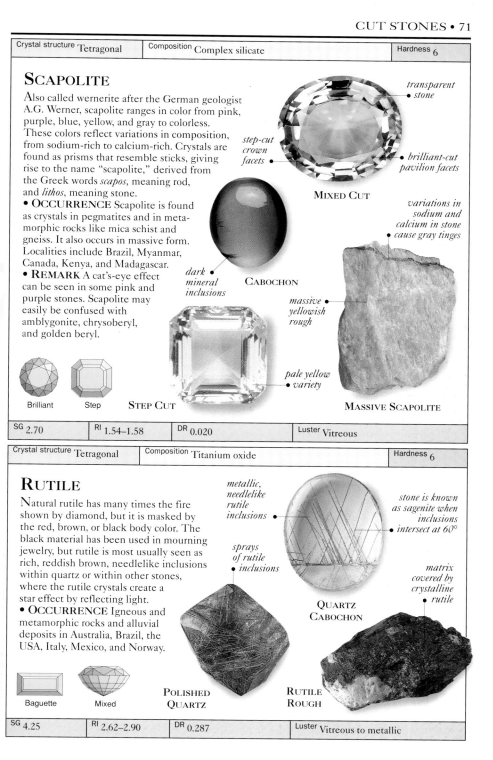

transparent stone

step-cut crown facets

brilliant-cut pavilion facets

MIXED CUT

variations in sodium and calcium in stone cause gray tinges

dark mineral inclusions

CABOCHON

massive yellowish rough

pale yellow variety

Brilliant   Step   **STEP CUT**

MASSIVE SCAPOLITE

| SG 2.70 | RI 1.54–1.58 | DR 0.020 | Luster Vitreous |

| Crystal structure Tetragonal | Composition Titanium oxide | Hardness 6 |

RUTILE

Natural rutile has many times the fire shown by diamond, but it is masked by the red, brown, or black body color. The black material has been used in mourning jewelry, but rutile is most usually seen as rich, reddish brown, needlelike inclusions within quartz or within other stones, where the rutile crystals create a star effect by reflecting light.
• **OCCURRENCE** Igneous and metamorphic rocks and alluvial deposits in Australia, Brazil, the USA, Italy, Mexico, and Norway.

metallic, needlelike rutile inclusions

stone is known as sagenite when inclusions intersect at 60°

sprays of rutile inclusions

matrix covered by crystalline rutile

QUARTZ CABOCHON

Baguette   Mixed

POLISHED QUARTZ

RUTILE ROUGH

| SG 4.25 | RI 2.62–2.90 | DR 0.287 | Luster Vitreous to metallic |

Crystal structure Tetragonal	Composition Zirconium silicate	Hardness 7½

ZIRCON

Zircon is most famous for its colorless stones, which closely resemble diamonds and have been used both intentionally and mistakenly in their place. Although colorless when pure, impurities will produce yellow, orange, blue, red, brown, and green varieties. Brown stones from Thailand, Vietnam, and Kampuchea are usually heat treated to change them into the colorless or blue stones popular in jewelry. Blue stones that revert to brown will regain the blue if reheated. Blue zircon reheated in the presence of oxygen will change to golden yellow. Zircon may be distinguished from diamond by its double refraction and by wear and tear on its facet edges. It has been imitated by both colorless glass and synthetic spinel. Some zircon contains radioactive thorium and uranium, which eventually break down the crystal structure. Decayed stones are known as "low" zircon, with a "metamict" structure; undamaged material is "high" zircon.
• OCCURRENCE Gem-quality crystals are usually found as pebbles in alluvial deposits. Sri Lanka has been a source of gem material for over 2,000 years; other localities include Myanmar, Thailand, Cambodia, Vietnam, Kampuchea, Australia, Brazil, Nigeria, Tanzania, and France.
• REMARK Zircon was believed to provide the wearer with wisdom, honor, and riches, and loss of luster was said to warn of danger. The name is from the Arabic *zargun*, which derives from the Persian for "gold color."

• *colorless zircon produced by heating reddish brown material*

RECTANGULAR STEP CUT

green stones are often decayed "low" zircon

waterworn pebble with polished surface

OVAL BRILLIANT CUT

GREEN "METAMICT" PEBBLE

natural golden • yellow color

zircon crystal •

OVAL MIXED CUT

• golden brown is most popular color for zircon jewelry

• pegmatite matrix

• dark biotite mica

CUSHION BRILLIANT CUT　　**CRYSTALS IN MATRIX**

SG 4.69	RI 1.93–1.98	DR 0.059	Luster Resinous to adamantine

doubling of back facets

stone heat treated to achieve blue color

ROUND BRILLIANT CUT

uneven color distribution

yellowish reflections

ROUND BRILLIANT CUT

smooth surface

WATERWORN PEBBLES

green zircon may have "metamict" structure

doubling of back facets

untreated reddish brown color

RECTANGULAR STEP CUT

dark golden brown stone

crown facets

CUSHION BRILLIANT CUT

double pyramidal ends

ZIRCON RINGS
Its adamantine luster, strong birefraction, hardness, and vast color range make zircon an attractive stone when set in a ring. Unfortunately, its use is restricted by its brittle nature; cutting is difficult and the cut stone is easily damaged.

leaf green mixed-cut zircon

square cross section

yellow zircon in center, flanked by pale blue-violet stones

TETRAGONAL ZIRCON CRYSTAL

Brilliant

Cushion

Zircon

Baguette

Mixed

Crystal structure Tetragonal	Composition Calcium aluminum silicate	Hardness 6½

VESUVIANITE

This mineral was first discovered on the Italian volcano Vesuvius as small, perfect crystals. Also called idocrase, it may be red, yellow, green, brown, or purple. It is seldom used in jewelry, but it may be cut for collectors. Crystals are usually thick prisms with a square cross section.
• **OCCURRENCE** There are several varieties: californite from California is green; rare blue cyprine is found in Norway; yellowish green xanthite is from New York; green wiluite crystals are from the former USSR. Other localities include Austria, Canada, Italy, and Switzerland.
• **REMARK** Vesuvianite may be confused with demantoid garnet, diopside, epidote, smoky quartz, tourmaline, zircon, and peridot.

polished massive material

yellowish green variety

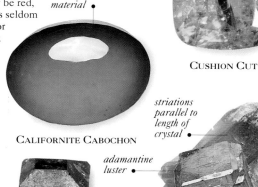

CUSHION CUT

CALIFORNITE CABOCHON

striations parallel to length of crystal

adamantine luster

tetragonal prism with smooth faces

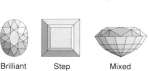

Brilliant   Step   Mixed

VESUVIANITE CRYSTAL   VESUVIANITE CRYSTALS

SG 3.40	RI 1.70–1.75	DR 0.005	Luster Vitreous to adamantine

Crystal structure Tetragonal	Composition Sodium aluminum beryllium silicate	Hardness 6

TUGTUPITE

Tugtupite was first discovered in 1960 in Greenland, where it is carved for jewelry. Colors include dark red to bright pink and shades of orange. It may look mottled. When it is placed in the dark, the paler parts of the rock fade to white, but exposure to light restores the color.
• **OCCURRENCE** Tugtupite is found as massive opaque material in pegmatite veins. It also occurs in northern Russia.
• **REMARK** The name derives from its occurrence in Tugtup, Greenland, and means "reindeer stone."

white albite feldspar associated with tugtupite

deep pink brought out by polishing surface

pink tugtupite

POLISHED STONE

intergrown albite feldspar

TUGTUPITE ROUGH

Cabochon   Cameo   Polished

SG 2.40	RI 1.49–1.50	DR 0.006	Luster Vitreous

Crystal structure Hexagonal	Composition Beryllium aluminum silicate	Hardness 7½

EMERALD (BERYL)

Emerald derives its beautiful green color from the presence of chromium and vanadium. Emeralds are rarely flawless, so stones are often oiled to fill and disguise cracks, hide flaws, and enhance color. To minimize the loss of material, the step cut (also called the emerald cut) is commonly used, but ancient engravings are known, and cameos, intaglios, and beads can make the best of a flawed stone.

• **OCCURRENCE** Found in granites, pegmatites, and schists, as well as alluvial deposits, the finest emeralds are from Colombia. Other sources are Austria, India, Australia, Brazil, South Africa, Egypt, the USA, Norway, Pakistan, and Zimbabwe.

• **REMARK** Most emeralds used in historical jewelry were from Cleopatra's mines in Egypt, which now yield only poor-quality emeralds.

inclusions make stone look cloudy

PENDELOQUE

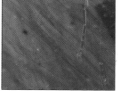

Tremolite inclusions may be found in emeralds as short rods or long fibers.

unusual domed front

group of inclusions

stone is semi-translucent

OCTAGONAL CABOCHON

POLISHED PEBBLE

Synthetic emeralds have characteristic veil or wisp-like, liquid-filled inclusions.

cracks and inclusions common in emerald

brilliant-cut crown facets

good emerald-green color

scratched prism face

MIXED CUT

crystals often found worn or etched

white calcite crystals

prism has flat ends

SYNTHETIC PENDELOQUE

HEXAGONAL CRYSTAL

Pendeloque	Step	Step	Cabochon

CRYSTAL IN MATRIX

SG 2.71	RI 1.57–1.58	DR 0.006		Luster Vitreous

Crystal structure Hexagonal	Composition Beryllium aluminum silicate	Hardness 7½

AQUAMARINE (BERYL)

In the 19th century the preferred color for aquamarine was sea green, and indeed the name itself means seawater. Today the most valued colors are sky blue and dark blue. Aquamarine is dichroic, appearing blue or colorless as the stone is viewed from different angles. Gem-quality aquamarine is found as hexagonal crystals, which may be up to 39 in (1 m) long and flawless, with striations along the length of the crystal. Aquamarine is often cut with the table facet parallel to the length of the crystal in order to emphasize the deepest coloration.

• **OCCURRENCE** The best of the gem-quality aquamarine is found in Brazil, where it occurs in pegmatites and alluvial deposits of gravel, locally called *cascalho*. Other localities include the Urals (Russia), Afghanistan, Pakistan, India, and, more recently exploited, Nigeria. A dark blue variety occurs in Madagascar.

• **REMARK** Almost all aquamarine on the market has been heat treated to enhance its color. Care must be taken not to overheat the stones, as they may become colorless.

untreated, sky blue stone

OCTAGONAL STEP CUT

cat's-eye effect visible on cabochon

fibrous habit

CABOCHON

step cut typical for aquamarine *heat treatment has lightened color*

OCTAGONAL STEP CUT

untreated stone has greenish tinge

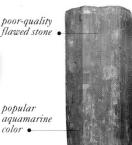

OCTAGONAL STEP CUT

many small facets

BRILLIANT CUT

crystal is too green and will require heat treatment

poor-quality flawed stone

popular aquamarine color

AQUAMARINE CRYSTALS

Brilliant   Step Cabochon

SG 2.69	RI 1.57–1.58	DR 0.006	Luster Vitreous

| Crystal structure Hexagonal | Composition Beryllium aluminum silicate | Hardness 7½ |

HELIODOR (BERYL)

Heliodor, a yellow or golden yellow form of beryl, has always been linked with the sun. Gem-quality specimens are occasionally found, but more often inclusions of fine, slender tubes are present that are visible to the naked eye.
• OCCURRENCE Heliodor is found associated with aquamarine in granitic pegmatites. The finest quality stones are found in the Urals (Russia). Brazilian heliodor is often a pale yellow and is step cut to give depth of color. Heliodor from Madagascar is a finer color. Other localities include the Ukraine, Namibia, and the USA.

glowing, golden yellow color •

SCISSORS CUT

heart-shaped cut keeps maximum possible weight •

bevel-edged crystal with flat ends •

FANCY CUT

Marquise   Table   Baguette

HELIODOR CRYSTALS IN MATRIX

| SG 2.80 | RI 1.57–1.58 | DR 0.005 | Luster Vitreous |

| Crystal structure Hexagonal | Composition Beryllium aluminum silicate | Hardness 7½ |

GOSHENITE (BERYL)

Goshenite is the pure, colorless variety of beryl. It has been used to imitate diamond or emerald, by placing silver or green-colored metal foil behind a cut goshenite gemstone, then placing the stone in a closed setting so that the foil cannot be detected.
• OCCURRENCE Goshenite is named after Goshen, Massachusetts, where it was first found. Present localities include Canada, Brazil, and the former USSR.
• REMARK Pale and colorless beryl was once used for the lenses in spectacles, thus the German word for spectacles, *brille*, may have been derived from the word "beryl."

• *stones are transparent*

vitreous luster •

FANCY CUT

crystals have hexagonal outline •

spiky inclusions are common •

Brilliant   Step   Mixed

BRILLIANT CUT

TABULAR CRYSTAL

| SG 2.80 | RI 1.58–1.59 | DR 0.008 | Luster Vitreous |

Crystal structure Hexagonal	Composition Beryllium aluminum silicate	Hardness 7½

MORGANITE (BERYL)

Colored by manganese impurities, the pink, rose, peach, and violet varieties of beryl are called morganite, after banker and gem enthusiast, J. Pierpoint Morgan. Morganite tends to occur as short and stubby (tabular) prisms and is dichroic, showing either two shades of the body color or one shade and colorless.

• **OCCURRENCE** The first morganite to be described was a pale rose-colored specimen from California, where it occurred with tourmaline. Some of the finest morganite is from Madagascar; Brazil produces pure pink crystals, as well as some containing aquamarine and morganite in the same crystal. Other localities include Elba (Italy), Mozambique, Namibia, Zimbabwe, and (recently discovered) Pakistan.

• **REMARK** Stones with a yellow or orange tinge may be heat treated for a purer pink.

• *typical pale pink color*

many small • facets

OVAL MIXED CUT

vitreous • luster

BRILLIANT CUT

DROP-SHAPED CUT

pink color from manganese •

liquid-filled inclusions •

ROUND BRILLIANT CUT

Brilliant   Step

MORGANITE ROUGH

SG 2.80	RI 1.58–1.59	DR 0.008	Luster Vitreous

Crystal structure Hexagonal	Composition Beryllium aluminum silicate	Hardness 7½

RED BERYL

Very rare, and seldom seen as a cut stone, red beryl nonetheless has an unusually intense color, due to the presence of manganese.

• **OCCURRENCE** Found in rhyolites in the Thomas Mountains and Wah Wah Mountains in Utah.

• **REMARK** Red beryl is also called bixbite (not to be confused with bixbyite, a manganese iron oxide).

prismatic red beryl crystal •

rhyolite • matrix

Brilliant

CRYSTAL IN MATRIX

SG 2.80	RI 1.58–1.59	DR 0.008	Luster Vitreous

Crystal structure Hexagonal	Composition Calcium phosphate	Hardness 5

APATITE

With a value of only 5 on the Mohs scale of hardness, apatite is seldom faceted as a gemstone, except for collectors. However, when cut correctly, stones are bright with strong colors. Transparent to opaque, apatite occurs as colorless, yellow, blue, violet, or green hexagonal prisms or tabular crystals.

• **OCCURRENCE** Apatite is an abundant mineral found in many types of rock, but most gem-quality material is associated with pegmatites. Blue apatite from Myanmar is strongly dichroic, showing colorless or blue when viewed from different directions. Fibrous blue apatite from Myanmar and Sri Lanka may be cut *en cabochon* to show a cat's-eye. Chatoyant stones are also found in Brazil, along with yellow, blue, and green varieties. Other localities include the Kola Peninsula (Russia), Canada, East Africa, Sweden, Spain, and Mexico.

• **REMARK** Spanish apatite is often called "asparagus stone," because of its yellowish green color.

blue-gray fibrous apatite

CAT'S-EYE CABOCHON

black inclusions

ROUND BRILLIANT CUT

chipped facet edge, due to brittleness of stone

OCTAGONAL STEP CUT

gray-green color

OCTAGONAL STEP CUT

stones are opaque to transparent

CUSHION MIXED CUT

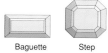
cut stones are bright and strongly colored

RECTANGULAR STEP CUT

pyramidal end

yellow hexagonal prism

APATITE CRYSTAL

colorless apatite crystal

quartz and gibertite matrix

APATITE CRYSTALS IN MATRIX

Baguette

Step

Step

Cabochon

SG 3.20	RI 1.63–1.64	DR 0.003	Luster Vitreous

Crystal structure Hexagonal	Composition Beryllium magnesium aluminum oxide	Hardness 8

TAAFFEITE

Taaffeite is very rare, and is unique in that it is the only gemstone not recognized as a new mineral species until it had been faceted. The first specimen (see right) was found by Count Taaffe in Ireland, in a jeweler's box of stones. It looked like spinel, had a pale mauve tinge, and was cushion cut, but was eventually found to be a new, doubly refractive (rather than singly refractive like spinel) mineral. Since then, more specimens have been found; these range in hue from red to blue to almost colorless.
• **OCCURRENCE** Taaffeite occurs in Sri Lanka, China, and the former USSR.
• **REMARK** No imitation taaffeites appear to exist.

• *first specimen to be identified*

• *grayish mauve color*

CUSHION CUT

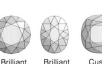

transparent • stone

semi-translucent pebble •

vitreous luster •

ROUND BRILLIANT CUT

TAAFFEITE ROUGH

 Brilliant Brilliant Cushion

SG 3.61	RI 1.72–1.77	DR 0.004	Luster Vitreous

Crystal structure Hexagonal	Composition Barium titanium silicate	Hardness 6½

BENITOITE

The blue crystals of benitoite were discovered in 1906 by a mineral prospector who mistook them for sapphires. Crystals are shaped like flattened triangles and have a strong dispersion similar to diamond, but this is masked by the color. Dichroism is strong: the stone appears blue or colorless when viewed from different angles. Colorless crystals occur but are rarely faceted.
• **OCCURRENCE** Crystals occur in veins in blue schists. The sole source is in San Benito County, California, after which the stone is named.

appears colorless at certain angles •

pyramidal • end

BRILLIANT CUT

• *unevenly distributed color*

BRILLIANT CUT

blue benitoite • crystals

conchoidal • fracture

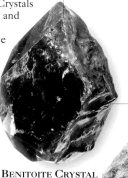

BENITOITE CRYSTAL FRAGMENT

BENITOITE CRYSTALS IN MATRIX

 Brilliant Brilliant Cushion

SG 3.67	RI 1.76–1.80	DR 0.047	Luster Vitreous

Crystal structure Trigonal	Composition Silicon dioxide	Hardness 7

ROCK CRYSTAL (QUARTZ)

Colorless and transparent, rock crystal is the most widely distributed variety of quartz, one of the most common minerals of the Earth's crust. The crystals are usually found as colorless hexagonal prisms, with pyramidal ends and striations perpendicular to their length; they are often twinned. Cleavage is poor and fracture conchoidal.

• **OCCURRENCE** Although found worldwide, the most important sources of rock crystal are in Brazil. Other localities include the Swiss and French Alps, where fine crystals occur, and Madagascar, the former USSR, and the USA.

• **REMARK** The name "quartz" comes from the Greek word *krustallos*, meaning ice, because it was thought that quartz was ice formed by the gods. Since the Middle Ages, crystal balls made of rock crystal have been used to predict the future. Today, rock crystal is used in lamps, lenses, and the manufacture of glass and precision instruments. Synthetic rock crystal has been produced since 1950 for use in watches.

transparent stone

ROUND BRILLIANT CUT

facet edges may wear on older stones

vitreous luster

CUSHION BRILLIANT CUT

drilled hole

carved grooves

POLISHED BEAD

POLISHED ROCK CRYSTAL
This flat disk of polished rock crystal has been engraved and set with an enameled monogram of blue, black, and gold.

colorless through yellowish shading

striations on prism faces

pyramidal ends

hexagonal crystals

Bead

Cameo

Brilliant

Step

SINGLE CRYSTAL

CRYSTALS

SG 2.65	RI 1.54–1.55	DR 0.009	Luster Vitreous

Crystal structure Trigonal	Composition Silicon dioxide	Hardness 7

AMETHYST (QUARTZ)

Crystalline quartz in shades of purple, lilac, or mauve is called amethyst, a stone traditionally worn to guard against drunkenness and to instill a sober and serious mind. Amethyst is dichroic, showing a bluish or reddish purple tinge when viewed from different angles. Usually faceted as a mixed or step cut, amethyst has distinctive inclusions that look like tigerstripes, thumbprints, or feathers. Some amethyst is heat treated to change the color to yellow, producing citrine (see opposite). Crystals that are part citrine and part amethyst are called ametrine.
• **OCCURRENCE** Amethyst is found in alluvial deposits or in geodes. Some of the largest geodes containing amethyst are in Brazil. Amethyst from the Urals (Russia) has a reddish tinge; Canadian amethyst is violet. Other localities include Sri Lanka, India, Uruguay, Madagascar, the USA, Germany, Australia, Namibia, and Zambia.
• **REMARK** Poor quality material is often tumbled to make beads. If a stone is pale it may be set in a closed setting or have foil placed behind it to enhance the color. Amethyst has been imitated by glass and synthetic corundum.

Characteristic tigerstripe inclusions are caused by parallel, liquid-filled canals.

TIE PIN
Amethyst jewelry was popular in the late 19th century. This handsome gold tie pin is adorned with an octagonal step-cut amethyst.

typical • purplish violet color

OVAL MIXED CUT

color darkens toward tip of • amethyst crystal

purple stone • from Russia

polished, convex front

alternate colors due to twinning •

HEXAGONAL MIXED CUT

slice cut • perpendicular to length of crystal

AMETHYST CRYSTAL SLICE

AMETHYST CRYSTALS ASSOCIATED WITH ROCK CRYSTAL

Baguette

Bead

Mixed

SG 2.65	RI 1.54–1.55	DR 0.009	Luster Vitreous

Crystal structure Trigonal	Composition Silicon dioxide	Hardness 7

CITRINE (QUARTZ)

Citrine is the yellow or golden yellow variety of quartz. The yellow coloration, due to the presence of iron, is also responsible for the name, derived from the word *citrus*. Natural citrine is usually a pale yellow, but rare; most citrine on the market is heat-treated amethyst (see opposite).

• **OCCURRENCE** Gem-quality citrine is extremely rare. The best material is found in Brazil, Spain, Madagascar, and the former USSR.

• **REMARK** Citrine has been used to imitate topaz (see pp.106–107) and was once called Brazilian topaz.

orange tinge often seen in citrine •

MIXED CUT

yellow color due to presence of iron

MIXED CUT PENDELOQUE

pyramidal end •

Brilliant   Pendeloque   Cabochon

CITRINE CRYSTAL

SG 2.65	RI 1.54–1.55	DR 0.009	Luster Vitreous

Crystal structure Trigonal	Composition Silicon dioxide	Hardness 7

ROSE QUARTZ

Pink or peach-colored quartz is called rose quartz and is mainly used in decorative carvings. Its color is thought to be due to the presence of small amounts of titanium. Crystals of rose quartz are very rare; more usually, massive lumps are found, which can be carved or cut *en cabochon* or as beads. Transparent material is uncommon; it is usually cloudy or cracked, partly because it is so brittle. Rutile inclusions in rose quartz may produce a star effect when the stone is cut *en cabochon*.

• **OCCURRENCE** Rose quartz is found in pegmatites. The best material is from Madagascar, but Brazil produces a greater quantity. Other sites are the USA (Colorado), the former USSR, Scotland, and Spain.

ROSE QUARTZ SEAL
Intaglio seals such as this, made with an incised rather than a raised design, were very popular in ancient Rome.

pale pink stone from Madagascar

rose quartz crystals •

BRILLIANT CUT

crystals are typically cloudy •

Bead   Mixed   Cameo

ROSE QUARTZ CRYSTALS

SG 2.65	RI 1.54–1.55	DR 0.009	Luster Vitreous

Crystal structure Trigonal	Composition Silicon dioxide	Hardness 7

BROWN QUARTZ

Brown quartz includes crystalline quartz of a light brown or dark brown color, grayish brown "smoky" quartz, and the black variety called morion. Brown or smoky quartz from the Cairngorm Mountains of Scotland is called cairngorm. When irradiated, colorless quartz may change color to grayish brown, suggesting that brown quartz may have been formed by natural radiation within the ground. Brown quartz crystals are hexagonal prisms with pyramidal ends, in which inclusions of the mineral rutile may be present.

• **OCCURRENCE** Crystals weighing as much as 650 lb (300 kg) have been found in Brazil. Other localities include Madagascar, the Swiss Alps, the USA (Colorado), Australia, and Spain.

• **REMARK** Much of the smoky quartz on the market is in fact irradiated rock crystal. Brown quartz has been confused with andalusite, axinite, idocrase, and brown tourmaline.

• *color may be due to natural irradiation*

FANCY-CUT SMOKY QUARTZ

vitreous luster •

characteristic grayish brown color •

BRILLIANT-CUT SMOKY QUARTZ

pyramidal end •

SNUFF BOTTLE
Like most varieties of quartz, smoky quartz may be polished and fashioned in many ways. This snuff bottle, with red stopper and spoon, is of Chinese origin.

opaque hexagonal prism •

horizontal striations on prism face •

MORION CRYSTAL

INTAGLIO SEAL
This incised intaglio was carved in smoky quartz and has been set in a polished octagon of obsidian, which is a natural volcanic glass. Intaglio seals were popular with the ancient Romans. This piece depicts a Roman wearing a helmet.

incised image •

polishing of one facet makes interior visible •

Mixed   Cameo   *smoky quartz intaglio*

WATERWORN CAIRNGORM PEBBLE

SG 2.65	RI 1.54–1.55	DR 0.009	Luster Vitreous

Crystal structure Trigonal	Composition Silicon dioxide	Hardness 7

AVENTURINE QUARTZ

This form of quartz contains inclusions of small crystals that reflect light and give a range of colors – depending on the nature of the inclusion. Green aventurine quartz has platy inclusions of green fuchsite mica; pyrite inclusions give a brown color; a greenish brown color may be due to the mineral goethite. Other inclusions result in bluish white, bluish green, or orange varieties.

- **OCCURRENCE** Aventurine quartz is found in Brazil, India, and Russia. Other localities include the USA, Japan, and Tanzania.
- **REMARK** Aventurine quartz has been confused with aventurine feldspar, amazonite, and jade. A simulant known as goldstone has been made to imitate both aventurine quartz and aventurine feldspar. It contains small triangles and hexagons of copper held in glass. With a 10x hand lens it should be possible to see the outlines of the copper spangles.

• *brassy yellow mica inclusions*

• *oval orange-brown cabochon*

CABOCHON

• *fuchsite mica inclusions give green color*

POLISHED SLAB

The copper inclusions in goldstone are visible with a 10x hand lens.

cryptocrystalline quartz with light-reflecting inclusions •

AVENTURINE QUARTZ ROUGH

Cabochon   Cameo   Polished

SG 2.65	RI 1.54–1.55	DR 0.009	Luster Vitreous

Crystal structure Trigonal	Composition Silicon dioxide	Hardness 7

MILKY QUARTZ

This form of quartz derives its distinctive milky white or cream color from inclusions of gas and liquid bubbles. The degree of milkiness depends on the number and size of inclusions present. Crystals are hexagonal prisms with pyramidal ends.

- **OCCURRENCE** Very large crystals are found in Siberia. Other localities include Brazil, the European Alps, Madagascar, the USA, and Namibia.
- **REMARK** When polished or cut *en cabochon*, it may be confused with opal.

milkiness due to gas and liquid inclusions •

double pyramidal ends •

OVAL CUSHION CUT

Brilliant   Cameo

HEXAGONAL CRYSTAL

SG 2.65	RI 1.54–1.55	DR 0.009	Luster Vitreous

Crystal structure Trigonal	Composition Silicon dioxide	Hardness 7

CHATOYANT QUARTZ

The three varieties of quartz described here all have a fibrous structure, with inclusions of crocidolite (blue asbestos) that cause a cat's-eye effect known as chatoyancy. This effect is best seen when the stones are cut *en cabochon*. Each stone displays different colors according to the exact nature of the inclusions. The grayish yellow, semitranslucent appearance of quartz cat's-eye is due to inclusions of crocidolite "asbestos" and, less commonly, hornblende. It has a silky luster. "Tiger's-eye" is black, with iron oxide staining that gives yellow and golden brown stripes. "Hawk's-eye" forms when crocidolite changes to quartz, but the blue-gray or blue-green color of the original material remains.

• OCCURRENCE Quartz cat's-eye comes from Sri Lanka, India, and Brazil. The most important source of tiger's-eye is in South Africa, where it is found in thick slabs, together with the less common hawk's-eye. Chatoyant quartz is also found in Australia and the USA.

• REMARK Chatoyant quartz is always called *quartz* cat's-eye to avoid confusion with other chatoyant gems, particularly chrysoberyl.

wavy, fibrous • structure

markings resemble • tigerstripes

TIGER'S-EYE POLISHED SLAB

• yellow-brown stripes due to iron oxide staining

POLISHED TIGER'S-EYE

original blue color and fibrous structure retained •

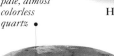

HAWK'S-EYE ROUGH

pale, almost colorless quartz •

cabochon cut brings out cat's-eye effect

waterworn fragment exhibits fibrous • structure

HAWK'S-EYE CIGARETTE BOX
In this attractive ornament, made of polished slices of blue hawk's-eye, the wavy, fibrous nature of the original asbestos can be clearly seen. Partial oxidation has created a few yellow waves.

QUARTZ CAT'S-EYE CABOCHON

rough displays no chatoyancy •

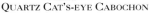

QUARTZ CAT'S-EYE ROUGH

Bead   Cabochon   Polished

SG 2.65	RI 1.54–1.55	DR 0.009	Luster Vitreous

Crystal structure Trigonal	Composition Silicon dioxide	Hardness 7

QUARTZ WITH INCLUSIONS

Quartz specimens with mineral inclusions are very common and make attractive gemstones. "Rutilated quartz" or "sagenite," popularly known as Venus-hair stone, is quartz with needlelike rutile crystals. These may be red, black, or brassy yellow and have a metallic luster. "Tourmalinated quartz" has inclusions of black tourmaline, which form prismatic or needlelike crystals. Opaque, metallic yellow inclusions of gold are found in specimens of "gold quartz." Inclusions of silver may also be found within quartz, often in branchlike dendrites, and are silvery gray or black, opaque, and metallic. The iron minerals, goethite and pyrite, are also found as inclusions. If cut *en cabochon*, quartz containing goethite may show the cat's-eye effect.
• OCCURRENCE Quartz with inclusions is found in Madagascar, Brazil, South Africa, India, Sri Lanka, Germany, and Switzerland.

PERFUME BOTTLE
This piece of quartz contains distinctive inclusions of black, needlelike tourmaline crystals. It has been shaped, hollowed out, and polished to make a bottle.

• *needlelike tourmaline inclusions*

reddish brown rutile inclusions •

hexagonal quartz prisms •

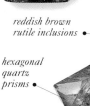

RUTILATED QUARTZ CRYSTALS IN MATRIX

Brilliant Bead Cabochon Cameo

SG 2.65	RI 1.54–1.55	DR 0.009	Luster Vitreous

Crystal structure Trigonal	Composition Silicon dioxide	Hardness 7

FIRE AGATE (CHALCEDONY)

Fire agate belongs to the chalcedony family of microcrystalline quartzes. These stones are either solid colored or have bands or mosslike or dendritic inclusions (agates). The distinctive iridescent colors of fire agate are caused by layers of iron oxide within the quartz. This rainbow effect may be brought out by cutting *en cabochon*.
• OCCURRENCE Fire agate is found in the USA (Arizona) and Mexico.
• REMARK Iris quartz has a similar iridescence, but this is caused by internal cracks.

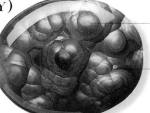

• *iridescence brought out by cabochon cut*

• *iron oxide inclusions give "oily" effect*

FIRE AGATE CABOCHON

rainbow colors •

POLISHED FIRE AGATE PEBBLE

Bead Cabochon Mixed Cameo

SG 2.61	RI 1.53–1.54	DR 0.004	Luster Vitreous

Crystal structure Trigonal	Composition Silicon dioxide	Hardness 7

AGATE (CHALCEDONY)

Agates occur in nodular masses in rocks such as volcanic lavas. When split open, they reveal an amazing variety of colors and patterns and a distinct banding that distinguishes agate from other kinds of chalcedony (the compact, micro-crystalline variety of quartz). Band colors are determined by the differing impurities present, although, since it is porous, agate is often dyed or stained to enhance the natural color. Agate also occurs in several distinct forms. Fortification agate has angularly arranged bands resembling an aerial view of a fortress. Moss agate (or mocha stone) is translucent and colorless, white or gray, with dark, moss- or treelike (dendritic) inclusions. It is usually cut as a thin slab or polished as ornaments, brooches, or pendants. Petrified wood is fossilized wood that has had its organic matter replaced by agate.

• **OCCURRENCE** Probably the most famous area for agates is Idar-Oberstein in Germany, where agate has been collected since 1548. Most agate now comes from the huge deposits in Uruguay and Brazil. Moss agate occurs in the Hindustan area of India; also China and the USA. The most famous petrified wood is found in the Petrified Forest in Arizona. Agates are also found in Mexico, Madagascar, Italy, Egypt, India, China, and Scotland.

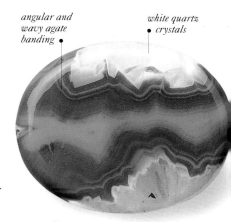

angular and wavy agate banding •

white quartz crystals •

STAINED AND POLISHED OVAL

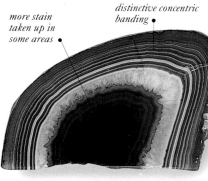

more stain taken up in some areas •

distinctive concentric banding •

STAINED AND POLISHED SLICE

parallel bands • and patterns

POLISHED SLICE

silica-rich • fluids give color to bands

• agate is often collected and polished by enthusiasts

agate forms in cavities in • volcanic rocks

AGATE ROUGH

SG 2.61	RI 1.53–1.54	DR 0.004	Luster Vitreous

iron oxides and hydroxides form tree-like inclusions •

LANDSCAPE AGATE

black dendritic inclusions •

inclusions appear to create a scenic • landscape

• pale cream background

green, mosslike inclusions •

white quartz crystals •

MOSS AGATE BROOCH STONE

MOSS AGATE ROUGH

when • magnified, bands in fortification agate resemble hill forts

colorless quartz crystals •

CARVED BOWL
Agate is a very popular stone for carving and polishing, although a piece as delicate as this bowl could be worked only by an expert lapidary. The parallel banding is typical of agate.

parallel • but angular banding

Cabochon   Cameo   Polished

FORTIFICATION AGATE ROUGH

Crystal structure Trigonal	Composition Silicon dioxide	Hardness 7

ONYX, SARD, AND SARDONYX (CHALCEDONY)

Onyx, sard, and sardonyx are all varieties of the microcrystalline quartz, chalcedony. Onyx is similar to agate (see pp.88–89), but it has straight rather than curved bands. These may be brown and white or black and white. Sard is a brownish red variety, also similar to agate. Sardonyx, a blend of sard and onyx, has the straight white bands of onyx and the brownish red of sard. All three varieties are carved as small sculptures and intaglios, or they may be polished, tumbled, or cut as beads. They are renowned as excellent materials for inlay work. Since ancient Egyptian times, onyx has been stained to improve or change its color. Much onyx has been produced by soaking agate in a sugar solution, then heating it in sulfuric acid to carbonize the sugar particles. Sard may be imitated by saturating chalcedony with an iron solution.

• **OCCURRENCE** Found worldwide, they are formed by the deposition of silica in gas cavities in lavas, which results in the distinctive bands.

• **REMARK** Onyx seals were very popular with the Romans, who carved the pattern of the seal in negative relief to give a raised print. They often used stones with several layers, each of a different color, which were then individually carved to produce a different pattern in each layer.

FLOWER CAMEO
This cameo was worked from a single piece of onyx. The dark, opaque layer has been carved away in the shape of a flower to reveal the pale layer beneath.

straight brown and white banding, characteristic • of onyx

STRAIGHT SEAL
The straight layers of onyx have been exposed to dramatic effect in this seal, an ornament popular with the Romans.

vitreous luster on • some surfaces

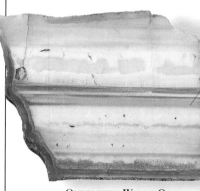

ONYX WITH WHITE OPAL

parallel bands of different colors •

POLISHED ONYX SLAB

Bead   Cabochon   Polished

SG 2.61	RI 1.53–1.54	DR 0.004	Luster Vitreous

stone is translucent, wth patchy color

characteristic brownish red color

OVAL POLISHED SARD

pitted, partly waterworn surface

dark, semi-translucent stone with waterworn surface

polished surface

SARD PEBBLE

SARD ROUGH

white and brownish red bands are characteristic of sardonyx

unbanded area is sard

unbanded chalcedony

sardonyx bands

POLISHED SARDONYX

SARDONYX CAMEO
In this intricately carved cameo, the pattern of a woman's head and winged dragon has been cut from three different layers – dark brown, white, and red-brown. A laurel garland is carved just inside the raised rim.

SARDONYX ROUGH

Crystal structure Trigonal	Composition Silicon dioxide	Hardness 7

CHRYSOPRASE/PRASE (CHALCEDONY)

Used by both the Greeks and Romans as a decorative stone, chrysoprase, a translucent, apple green stone, is the most valued variety of chalcedony. The color, derived from the presence of nickel, may fade in sunlight, and stones may then be confused with fine jade (see pp.124–125).

• **OCCURRENCE** Mines in Poland and Czechoslovakia once produced very fine chrysoprase. However, since 1965, the best quality material has come from Queensland (Australia). Other localities are Brazil, California, the Urals (Russia), and Austria.

• **REMARK** Another green chalcedony, prase, has a more somber hue and is very rare.

PRASE CAMEO
Set in gold as an ornamental pin, this piece of fine green prase has been carved and polished into a classically styled cameo.

fragments of • host rock

apple green • chrysoprase

CHRYSOPRASE ROUGH

Bead   Cabochon   Cameo

SG 2.61	RI 1.53–1.54	DR 0.004	Luster Vitreous to waxy

Crystal structure Trigonal	Composition Silicon dioxide	Hardness 7

JASPER (CHALCEDONY)

Jasper is a massive, fine-grained, opaque variety of chalcedony, believed to protect against sight defects and drought. It occurs in shades of brown, grayish blue, red, yellow, and green, and mixtures of these. "Orbicular" jasper has white or gray, eye-shaped patterns surrounded by red jasper. "Ribbon" jasper is striped and used in carvings, cameos, and intaglios, which show off its layered structure. Hornstone is a gray variety.

• **OCCURRENCE** Red jasper occurs in India and Venezuela; various colors occur in the USA, especially orbicular jasper in California; red and green ribbon jasper occurs in Russia. It also occurs in France and Germany.

stone may break easily at junction of stripes •

polished • surface

RIBAND JASPER FRAGMENT

mammillated • habit

iron oxide gives red coloring •

white quartz vein •

RED JASPER ROUGH

RED JASPER ROUGH

Cameo   Polished

SG 2.61	RI 1.53–1.54	DR 0.004	Luster Vitreous

Crystal structure Trigonal	Composition Silicon dioxide	Hardness 7

CARNELIAN (CHALCEDONY)

Also called cornelian, this translucent, reddish
orange variety of chalcedony was once
thought to still the blood and calm the
temper. Its various shades of red are due
to the presence of iron oxide. Stones may
be uniformly colored or faintly banded.
• **OCCURRENCE** The best carnelian
is from India, where it is placed in the
sun to change brown tints to red.
• **REMARK** Most carnelian on the
market is stained chalcedony from
Brazil or Uruguay.

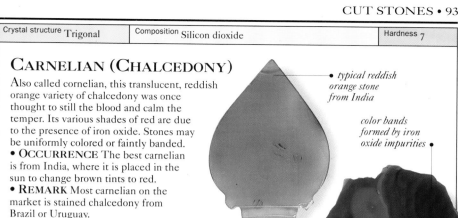

*typical reddish
orange stone
from India*

*color bands
formed by iron
oxide impurities*

POLISHED STONE

POLISHED CARNELIAN
FRAGMENT

Bead   Cabochon   Cameo

SG 2.61	RI 1.53–1.54	DR 0.004	Luster Vitreous to waxy

Crystal structure Trigonal	Composition Silicon dioxide	Hardness 7

BLOODSTONE AND PLASMA (CHALCEDONY)

Bloodstone (also called heliotrope) and
plasma are both opaque, green, spotted
varieties of chalcedony, used for decorative
carvings and cameos. The dark green of
bloodstone is spotted with red because
of the presence of iron oxides. These
distinctive spots seem to resemble blood,
giving the stone its name. Plasma is also
green and may have yellowish spots.
• **OCCURRENCE** India is the primary
source of bloodstone, but it also occurs
in Brazil, China, Australia, and the
USA. Plasma is mined in Zimbabwe.
• **REMARK** In the Middle Ages,
bloodstone was attributed with
special powers, as the spots were
thought to be the blood of Jesus
Christ. In Germany, hematite is
also called bloodstone, so this
variety is known as bluestone.

ROMAN CAMEO
The typical red
spotting in dark
green bloodstone
appears as an
almost solid mass
in the high relief
of this cameo.

*raised relief
carved from
red spotting*

*scattered
red spots
and veins*

*polished material
often used as inlay*

*very deep
green*

POLISHED
BLOODSTONE SLAB

PLASMA ROUGH

Bead   Cameo   Polished

SG 2.61	RI 1.53–1.54	DR 0.004	Luster Vitreous

Crystal structure Trigonal	Composition Aluminum oxide	Hardness 9

RUBY (CORUNDUM)

Ruby – the name given to red, gem-quality corundum – is one of the best gemstones for jewelry settings. Rubies may be any shade of red, from pinkish to purplish or brownish red, depending on the chromium and iron content of the stone. Frequent twinning of the crystals makes the material liable to fracture, yet ruby is a tough mineral, second only to diamond in hardness. Crystal prisms are hexagonal with tapering or flat ends. As the crystals grow, they form new layers, and, depending on the geological conditions and minerals present, color variations called zoning occur.

• **OCCURRENCE** Worldwide in igneous and metamorphic rocks, or as waterworn pebbles in alluvial deposits. The finest stones come from Myanmar; those from Thailand, the primary source, are brownish red; Afghanistan, Pakistan, and Vietnam yield bright red stones; those from India, the USA (North Carolina), Russia, Australia, and Norway are dark to opaque.

• **REMARK** In 1902, a Frenchman, Auguste Verneuil, produced a synthetic ruby crystal by exposing powdered aluminum oxide and coloring material to the flame of a blowtorch.

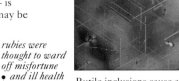

rubies were thought to ward off misfortune • and ill health

Rutile inclusions cause a silky appearance, which heat treatment will remove.

• *mixed cut is typical for rubies*

CUSHION MIXED CUT

star effect seen in cabochons when rutile • inclusions present

manufactured by • Verneuil method

stone • weighs over 138 carats

STEP-CUT SYNTHETIC

ROSSER REEVES RUBY

Color zoning indicates the layers of growth in a crystal. They can be seen here as a series of concentric hexagons, which appear parallel to the prismatic crystal faces.

purplish • red coloration

CABOCHON

pinkish red crystal •

largest gem-quality crystals are from Myanmar •

RUBY CRYSTAL

Brilliant	Step	Cabochon	Mixed

SG 4.00	RI 1.76–1.77	DR 0.008	Luster Vitreous

Crystal structure Trigonal	Composition Aluminum oxide	Hardness 9

SAPPHIRE (CORUNDUM)

All gem-quality corundum that is not red is called sapphire, yet this name is popularly associated with the color blue. Variation in color, due to iron and titanium impurities, spans many shades, but the most valuable is a clear, deep blue. Some stones, called "color-change sapphire," exhibit different shades of blue in artificial and natural light.

• **OCCURRENCE** Good-quality sapphire is found in Myanmar, Sri Lanka, and India. The best Indian sapphire is cornflower blue and is found in Kashmir, either in pegmatites or as waterworn pebbles in alluvial deposits. Sapphire from Thailand, Australia, and Nigeria is dark blue, and may appear nearly black. Montana produces sapphire of an attractive metallic blue. Other localities include Cambodia, Brazil, Kenya, Malawi, and Colombia.

• **REMARK** Synthetic sapphire production began in the late 19th century. Commercial quantities became available in the early 20th century.

• *rutile inclusions create 6-rayed star effect in cabochons*

STAR CABOCHON

pale blue Sri Lankan stone

CARVED BUDDHA
Since the Middle Ages, sapphire has symbolized the tranquility of the heavens, bestowing peace and amiability upon the wearer and suppressing wicked and impure thoughts.

BRILLIANT CUT

"Kashmir blue" crystals

sapphire crystal has intergrown with tourmaline

BLUE SAPPHIRE CRYSTAL

• *black tourmaline*

Brilliant   Cabochon   Cameo

SG 4.00	RI 1.76–1.77	DR 0.008	Luster Vitreous

Crystal structure Trigonal	Composition Aluminum oxide	Hardness 9

PADPARADSCHA (CORUNDUM)

Padparadscha is a very rare, pinkish orange sapphire. It is the only variety of corundum other than ruby that is given its own name, rather than being referred to as a sapphire of a particular color. The name derives from a Sinhalese word meaning "lotus blossom."

• **OCCURRENCE** Sri Lanka.

• **REMARK** Like all varieties of corundum, padparadscha is an excellent jewelry stone, second only to diamond in hardness.

characteristic pinkish orange color

vitreous luster

• *truncated heart shape*

MIXED CUT

Mixed

SG 4.00	RI 1.76–1.77	DR 0.008	Luster Vitreous

Crystal structure Trigonal	Composition Aluminum oxide	Hardness 9

COLORLESS SAPPHIRE (CORUNDUM)

The different colors found within members of the corundum group are due to small amounts of metal oxide impurities. Corundum without impurities (and therefore without color) is rare, but when found is classified as colorless sapphire. Stones made up of different colors, including colorless areas, are more common. Stones like these are generally oriented by the cutter so that the color is at the base. Then, when viewed from above, color fills the stone.
• **OCCURRENCE** Truly colorless sapphire is found in Sri Lanka. Cloudy or milky-colored sapphire is also found in Sri Lanka and referred to locally as *geuda*. Heat treatment of *geuda* produces blue sapphire, much of which is faceted and used in jewelry. Some Sri Lankan corundum shows red, blue, and colorless areas, which may be faceted or polished to give an interesting stone.
• **REMARK** Synthetic colorless corundum has been produced by the Verneuil method since about the 1920s and has been called diamondite.

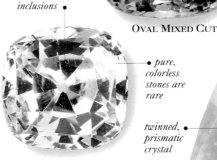

cabochon shows 6-rayed star •

near-colorless stone with grayish tinge •

STAR-STONE CABOCHON

elongated cut •

• colorless sapphire is free from impurities

bubblelike inclusions •

OVAL MIXED CUT

pyramidal end •

• pure, colorless stones are rare

twinned, prismatic crystal •

MIXED CUT

COLORLESS CRYSTAL

Brilliant   Brilliant   Cabochon

SG 4.00	RI 1.76–1.77	DR 0.008	Luster Vitreous

Crystal structure Trigonal	Composition Aluminum oxide	Hardness 9

GREEN SAPPHIRE (CORUNDUM)

From medieval times until the end of the 19th century, green sapphire was known as "oriental peridot." Many sapphires that appear green actually consist of very fine alternating bands of blue and yellow sapphire, which may be visible under a microscope.
• **OCCURRENCE** Green sapphires are found in Thailand, Sri Lanka, and Australia (Queensland and New South Wales).

very dark • green color

• vitreous luster

CUSHION CUT

Brilliant

SG 4.00	RI 1.76–1.77	DR 0.008	Luster Vitreous

Crystal structure Trigonal	Composition Aluminum oxide	Hardness 9

PINK SAPPHIRE (CORUNDUM)

Pure pink sapphire is colored by very small quantities of chromium, and with increasing amounts of chromium it forms a continuous color range with ruby. Tiny amounts of iron may produce pink-orange stones called padparadscha (see p.95), or iron and titanium impurities together may make a purplish stone. Pink sapphires are often cut with a deep profile.
• OCCURRENCE Pink sapphires, from a very pale and delicate pink to a near-red, occur in Sri Lanka, Myanmar, and East Africa.
• REMARK Like rubies (see p.94), pink sapphires are believed to ward off ill health and misfortune. For the wearer to gain the benefit of the stone, however, it has been thought necessary for it to be worn directly on the skin. Therefore stones are cut so that, when set in a piece of jewelry, the back makes contact with the skin.

• *pink color derives from chromium*

• *Sri Lankan stones range from pale pink to red*

CUSHION MIXED CUT

striations on • *crystal face*

stones may be worn next to the skin • *for maximum reputed benefit*

OVAL MIXED CUT

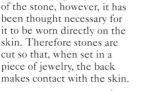

Brilliant   Cushion   Pendeloque

PINK SAPPHIRE CRYSTAL

SG 4.00	RI 1.76–1.77	DR 0.008	Luster Vitreous

Crystal structure Trigonal	Composition Aluminum oxide	Hardness 9

YELLOW SAPPHIRE (CORUNDUM)

Until the end of the 19th century, yellow sapphire was known as "oriental topaz" (only blue corundum was called sapphire). Nevertheless, yellow and greenish yellow sapphires make unusual and attractive gemstones in their own right.
• OCCURRENCE In Queensland and New South Wales (Australia), a greenish yellow sapphire is found that may be faceted. Similar stones occur in Thailand and pure yellow stones in Sri Lanka, the USA (Montana), and East Africa.

• *yellow sapphire, formerly known as oriental topaz*

CUSHION MIXED CUT

barrel-shaped crystal with • *tapering ends*

Brilliant

WATERWORN CRYSTAL

SG 4.00	RI 1.76–1.77	DR 0.008	Luster Vitreous

Crystal structure Trigonal	Composition Calcium carbonate	Hardness 3

CALCITE

Common worldwide, calcite is the principal component of limestones and marbles and of most stalactites and stalagmites. It can also be found as large, transparent, colorless, complex crystals, or as prismatic crystals intergrown with other minerals. Because of its softness it is faceted only for the collector, but marbles and brown, banded calcite from limestone caves are used for both decoration and carving.
• OCCURRENCE Italy is famous for fine-quality marbles, particularly the creamy Carrara marble. Transparent, colorless rhombs are known as "Iceland spar"; a white fibrous variety, cut *en cabochon*, shows the cat's-eye effect. Pink and green crystals occur in the USA, Germany, and England.

• *calcite crystals are highly birefractive*
• *vitreous luster on front, pearly luster at sides*
• *red tinge due to iron oxides*

"ICELAND SPAR" RHOMB

transparent, colorless crystals •

Step   Polished

PRISMATIC CALCITE CRYSTALS

SG 2.71	RI 1.48–1.66	DR 0.172	Luster Vitreous to pearly

Crystal structure Trigonal	Composition Beryllium silicate	Hardness 7½

PHENAKITE

Phenakite is a rare mineral found as white or colorless tabular crystals or stubby prisms. Twinning is common and distinguishes it from rock crystal (see p.81), with which it is often confused (hence its name, derived from the Greek word for "cheat"). Transparent crystals are faceted for the collector and are hard and bright.
• OCCURRENCE Phenakite occurs in pegmatites, granites, and mica schists. The best crystals are found in Brazil, the Urals (Russia), and the USA (Colorado). Other localities include Italy, Sri Lanka, Zimbabwe, and Namibia.
• REMARK A pebble weighing 1,470 carats was found in Sri Lanka and faceted to a 569-carat oval and several smaller stones.

• *phenakite has silvery look when cut well*
• *vitreous luster*

BRILLIANT CUT

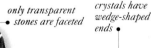
only transparent stones are faceted •
crystals have wedge-shaped ends •

BRILLIANT CUT

PHENAKITE CRYSTAL

Brilliant   Mixed

SG 2.96	RI 1.65–1.67	DR 0.015	Luster Vitreous

Crystal structure Trigonal	Composition Hydrated copper silicate	Hardness 5

DIOPTASE

Dioptase is a beautiful, vivid emerald green with a hint of blue. It has very high fire, but this is masked by its strong color, which may make stones translucent rather than transparent. Prized by the collector for its color, it is nonetheless rarely faceted, as stones are brittle and fragile, and too soft to be worn. It is sometimes confused with emerald.
• **OCCURRENCE** The best quality crystals are found in copper deposits in Russia, Namibia, Zaire, Chile, and the USA (Arizona).

crystals have perfect cleavage

emerald to bluish green coloration

DIOPTASE CRYSTALS

Brilliant   Cabochon

SG 3.31	RI 1.67–1.72	DR 0.053	Luster Vitreous

Crystal structure Trigonal	Composition Magnesium and calcium carbonate	Hardness 3½

DOLOMITE

Dolomite is found as colorless, white, pink, or yellow crystals, often with distinctive curved faces. Rarely faceted, because of its softness and perfect cleavage, its main use is in massive form, as a decorative stone.
• **OCCURRENCE** Found in limestones and marbles, the best crystals are from Italy, Switzerland, Germany, and the USA.

curved faces

colorless quartz

opaque dolomite crystals

TWIN CRYSTAL

TWINNED DOLOMITE CRYSTALS IN MATRIX

Step   Step

SG 2.85	RI 1.50–1.68	DR 0.179	Luster Vitreous to pearly

Crystal structure Trigonal	Composition Zinc carbonate	Hardness 5

SMITHSONITE

Smithsonite is usually found as bluish green or green botryoidal masses or soft layers, which are polished and used as an ornamental stone (sometimes called bonamite). It may also be colored pink by cobalt or yellow by cadmium. Crystals may also be found, but are faceted for the collector only.
• **OCCURRENCE** Colorless crystals in Namibia and Zambia; blue-green masses in the USA, Spain, and Greece; yellow in the USA and Sardinia.

blue smithsonite crust

opaque white smithsonite

SMITHSONITE ON MATRIX

pearly luster

SMITHSONITE ON MATRIX

Cabochon

SG 4.35	RI 1.62–1.85	DR 0.230	Luster Pearly

Crystal structure Trigonal	Composition Manganese carbonate	Hardness 4

RHODOCHROSITE

Rhodochrosite derives its pink color from manganese. Gem-quality crystals do occur and are cut for collectors, but the fine-grained, banded rock is more commonly used for decoration.
• **OCCURRENCE** Rhodochrosite occurs in veins associated with manganese, copper, silver, and lead deposits. Argentina has the oldest mines; its banded rhodochrosite is sometimes called "Inca rose." Today, the prime commercial sources are in the USA.

*alternate pink
• and red bands*

*• polished cross
section*

*pinkish red
crystals •*

**BANDED
RHODOCHROSITE**

**RHODOCHROSITE
CRYSTALS IN MATRIX**

Bead

Cabochon

Cameo

SG 3.60	RI 1.60–1.80	DR 0.220	Luster Vitreous to pearly

Crystal structure Trigonal	Composition Iron oxide	Hardness 6½

HEMATITE

Hematite usually occurs as massive, opaque material with a metallic luster, showing a blood red color when cut into thin slices. However, it can also occur as short, black, rhombohedral crystals and may have iridescent surfaces. When arranged like the petals of a flower, hematite is called an "iron rose." Shiny crystals may be called "specular" hematite, a name derived from their traditional use in mirrors.
• **OCCURRENCE** Main deposits are in igneous rocks around Lake Superior, Canada (Quebec), Brazil, Venezuela, and England. Iron roses are found in Switzerland and Brazil; cuttable material in England, Germany, and Elba.
• **REMARK** Powdered, it may be used as an artist's pigment or for polishing. In the past it was worn as protection against bleeding.

CARVED FROG
With a hardness of 6½, hematite is easily carved, but care must be taken to prevent scratching. This oriental-style frog has a gray metallic luster.

*shiny crystals
were once used
• as mirrors*

*play of light
• on surface*

"SPECULAR" HEMATITE

*"iron rose" •
arrangement
of crystals*

**IRIDESCENT
HEMATITE CRYSTALS**

Bead

Cabochon

Cameo

SG 5.20	RI 2.94–3.22	DR 0.280	Luster Metallic

Crystal structure	Composition	Hardness
Trigonal	Complex borosilicate	7½

RUBELLITE (TOURMALINE)

Members of the tourmaline family of minerals have the same basic crystal structure, but occur in many colors. Rubellite (from the Latin for red) is the name given to the pink or red variety, with ruby red stones the most highly prized. Rubellite crystals are striated, with a triangular cross section and a rounded outline. They may also occur with a fibrous habit, and show a cat's-eye when cut *en cabochon*.
- **OCCURRENCE** Russian pink and red tourmaline occurs in weathered granites. Other sites include Madagascar, the USA, Brazil, Myanmar, and East Africa.
- **REMARK** The specific gravity of tourmaline varies with color – dark red has a higher SG than pink.

dark pink color

fibrous habit visible in cat's-eye "flash"

CABOCHON

translucent stone

RECTANGULAR STEP CUT

rubellite crystals

rock crystal

RUBELLITE CRYSTALS IN MATRIX

Pendeloque   Step   Cabochon

SG	RI	DR	Luster
3.06	1.62–1.64	0.018	Vitreous

Crystal structure	Composition	Hardness
Trigonal	Complex borosilicate	7½

INDICOLITE (TOURMALINE)

Dark blue tourmaline is called indicolite or, occasionally, indigolite. Indicolite is often heat treated to lighten its color and produce a more attractive stone.
- **OCCURRENCE** An important source for indicolite is Siberia (Russia), where it occurs in yellow clays formed from weathered granites. Fine, bright blue tourmaline has recently been found in Paraiba, Brazil. Other localities include Madagascar and the USA.
- **REMARK** A lilac to violet blue or reddish blue variety (first found in Russia) is known as siberite.

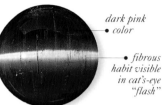

inky blue semi-translucent stone

greenish blue transparent stone from Brazil

OVAL MIXED CUT

RECTANGULAR STEP CUT

fractured surface

vertical striations

INDICOLITE CRYSTAL

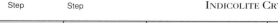

Step   Step

SG	RI	DR	Luster
3.06	1.62–1.64	0.018	Vitreous

Crystal structure Trigonal	Composition Complex borosilicate	Hardness 7½

DRAVITE (TOURMALINE)

Dravite is a very dark-colored (usually brown) form of tourmaline, rich in magnesium. It is possible to lighten the color by heat treatment. Dravite shows strong dichroism and should therefore be cut with the table facet parallel to the length of the crystal, in order to show a lighter and more attractive color.
• OCCURRENCE Dravite can occur as single crystals or as parallel or radiating groups. Brown tourmaline and yellow tourmaline occur together in the gem gravels of Sri Lanka. It is also found in the USA, Canada, Mexico, Brazil, and Australia.
• REMARK The name "dravite" is derived from the district of Drave, in Austria.

golden brown color

stones may be lightened by heat treatment

ROUND BRILLIANT CUT

orange-brown color

prismatic habit

opaque, dark brown crystal

Brilliant Brilliant Cushion

CUSHION MIXED CUT

CRYSTAL FRAGMENT

SG 3.06	RI 1.61–1.63	DR 0.018	Luster Vitreous

Crystal structure Trigonal	Composition Complex borosilicate	Hardness 7½

ACHROITE (TOURMALINE)

This particularly rare, colorless stone is a variety of elbaite, a member of the tourmaline group. It does not show the strong dichroism characteristic of most tourmaline varieties and therefore can be cut with the table facet either parallel or perpendicular to the length of the crystal. Colorless tourmaline may also be produced by applying heat to light pink tourmalines.
• OCCURRENCE Achroite occurs with colored tourmalines in the pegmatites of Madagascar and in the USA (Pala, California).
• REMARK Achroite is named after the Greek word *achroos*, meaning "without color."

transparent, colorless stone

girdle around "waist" of stone

ROUND BRILLIANT CUT

fracture is conchoidal

Brilliant Brilliant Mixed

OVAL BRILLIANT CUT

ACHROITE CRYSTAL

SG 3.06	RI 1.62–1.64	DR 0.018	Luster Vitreous

Crystal structure Trigonal	Composition Complex borosilicate	Hardness 7½

WATERMELON TOURMALINE

Tourmaline crystals with a pink center and a green rim, or vice versa, are called watermelon tourmaline, because their coloring is similar to the pink flesh and green rind of a watermelon. Many other tourmalines are made up of two or more colors, individual crystals containing up to 15 different colors or shades.
• **OCCURRENCE** Watermelon tourmaline is found in South Africa, Brazil, East Africa, and in many other localities.
• **REMARK** Parti- and multicolored tourmaline is carved or cut and polished to show off the different colors to best effect.

green and pink parts occur in single crystal

characteristic color zoning

Baguette

Cabochon

TABLE CUT

CRYSTAL SECTION

SG 3.06	RI 1.62–1.64	DR 0.018	Luster Vitreous

Crystal structure Trigonal	Composition Complex borosilicate	Hardness 7½

SCHORL (TOURMALINE)

Schorl is the black, iron-rich form of tourmaline and is very common. The opaque, prismatic crystals may be several yards in length.
• **OCCURRENCE** Found in pegmatites.
• **REMARK** During the Victorian era in Britain, black tourmaline was widely used for mourning jewelry, but today it has little, if any, value as a gemstone.

broken, worn end

vertical striations

Brilliant

Mixed

SCHORL CRYSTAL

SG 3.06	RI 1.62–1.67	DR 0.018	Luster Vitreous

Crystal structure Trigonal	Composition Complex borosilicate	Hardness 7½

GREEN AND YELLOW TOURMALINE

Yellow-green is the most common of all tourmaline color varieties, but emerald green is much rarer and more valuable. Indeed, until the 18th century it was often confused with emerald.
• **OCCURRENCE** Emerald green stones are found in Brazil, Tanzania, and Namibia; fibrous yellow material occurs in Sri Lanka.

semi-transparent stone

greenish yellow is most common color variety

Brilliant

BRILLIANT CUT

SG 3.06	RI 1.62–1.64	DR 0.018	Luster Vitreous

Crystal structure Orthorhombic	Composition Calcium carbonate	Hardness 3½

ARAGONITE

Aragonite is usually transparent or translucent and colorless or white when pure. Impurities may cause shades of yellow, blue, pink, or green to occur. It is found in many different habits: small, elongate, prismatic crystals form in radiating groups, and concretions and stalactites are also common. It has poor cleavage.

• **OCCURRENCE** Found mainly in sedimentary environments, aragonite may form as tufa (porous rock) in Czechoslovakia and Turkey. Other localities include Spain, France, the USA (Colorado), and Cumbria (England).

layering revealed in cut and polished section

crystals growing out of matrix

STALACTITIC POLISHED SLAB

crystals colorless when pure

Bead   Polished

CRYSTAL SPRAYS ON MATRIX

SG 2.94	RI 1.53–1.68	DR 0.155	Luster Vitreous

Crystal structure Orthorhombic	Composition Barium sulfate	Hardness 3

BARITE

Barite occurs in a variety of colors, including colorless, white, yellow, and blue, but its softness, perfect cleavage, brittleness, and high density make it of little use as a gemstone, and it is cut for collectors only. Crystals vary a great deal and may be transparent to opaque, with a variety of habits from tabular to massive.

• **OCCURRENCE** Barite is commonly found in lead and silver mines. It also occurs in limestones, and may be deposited by hot springs. Crystals up to 40 in (1 m) in length have been found in Cumbria, Cornwall, and Derbyshire, in England. Other good localities include Czechoslovakia, Romania, Germany, the USA, and Italy.

stones are faceted for collectors only

OCTAGONAL MIXED CUT

tabular, double-ended crystal

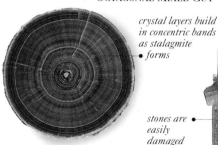

crystal layers build in concentric bands as stalagmite forms

STALAGMITE SECTION

stones are easily damaged

growth zones

BARITE CRYSTAL

Step   Mixed   Polished

SG 4.45	RI 1.63–1.65	DR 0.012	Luster Vitreous to pearly

Crystal structure Orthorhombic	Composition Strontium sulfate		Hardness 3½

CELESTINE

Celestine is usually found as colorless, milky white, yellow, orange, or pale blue prismatic crystals, or in fine-grained masses. With a hardness of only 3½ on the Mohs scale and perfect cleavage, celestine is extremely fragile. It has been cut for the collector, however, and some fine specimens can be seen in museums.

• **OCCURRENCE** Celestine may occur with sandstones or limestones, in evaporite deposits, in pegmatites, in cavities in volcanic rocks, or with galena and sphalerite in mineral veins. Most of the material that is capable of being faceted is found in either Namibia or Madagascar. It is also found in Italy (including Sicily), England, Czechoslovakia, the USA, and Canada.

colorless celestine is the most common • variety

cut stones are rare and • lack fire

MIXED CUT

transparent to semitranslucent colorless • crystal

sulfur matrix •

colorless celestine crystals •

Brilliant   Mixed

CELESTINE CRYSTAL

CRYSTALS IN MATRIX

SG 3.98	RI 1.62–1.63	DR 0.010	Luster Vitreous to pearly

Crystal structure Orthorhombic	Composition Lead carbonate		Hardness 3½

CERUSSITE

Cerussite is usually colorless, but white, gray, and black specimens have been found. Its two most distinctive features are its high density and its adamantine luster. Crystals have a stubby tabular or elongate habit. Cerussite is attractive, but it is too soft to have much value as a gemstone and is cut for collectors only.

• **OCCURRENCE** Cerussite is usually found around lead ores. Large, clear, transparent, colorless, cuttable crystals have been found in Tsumeb (Namibia). Other localities include Austria, Australia, Czechoslovakia, the USA, Germany, Scotland, and Italy, including Sardinia.

• **REMARK** Sometimes confused with diamond and other colorless gems, it may be distinguishable by its higher density.

• very pale gray color

worn facet edges • due to softness

ROUND BRILLIANT CUT

colorless, crystal "twin" •

surface formerly • attached to matrix

Brilliant   Brilliant

PRISMATIC CRYSTAL

SG 6.51	RI 1.80–2.08	DR 0.274	Luster Adamantine

Crystal structure Orthorhombic	Composition Aluminum fluorohydroxysilicate	Hardness 8

TOPAZ

Topaz occurs in a range of different colors: deep golden yellow topaz (sometimes called sherry topaz) and pink topaz are the most valuable; blue and green stones are also popular. Natural pink stones are rare – most pink topaz is heat treated yellow material. Much colorless topaz is irradiated and heat treated to a range of blues, some almost indistinguishable from aquamarine when seen with the naked eye. Some topaz has tear-shaped cavities, containing a gas bubble or several immiscible (nonmixing) liquids. Other inclusions such as cracks, streaks, and veils also occur. Prismatic topaz crystals have a characteristic lozenge-shaped cross section and striations parallel to their length. Topaz has one perfect cleavage.

• **OCCURRENCE** Topaz occurs in igneous rocks such as pegmatites, granites, and volcanic lavas. It may also be found in alluvial deposits as waterworn pebbles. Localities include Brazil, the USA, Sri Lanka, Myanmar, the former USSR, Australia, Tasmania, Pakistan, Mexico, Japan, and Africa. Brazil, Pakistan, and Russia are sources of pink topaz.

• **REMARK** In the 17th century the Braganza diamond (1,640 carats) in the Portuguese crown was thought to be the largest diamond ever found. This was never confirmed, and it is now believed to have been a colorless topaz. The name "topaz" is thought to be derived from the Sanskrit word *tapas*, meaning fire.

pale yellow topaz

stones up to 35,000 carats have been faceted

OVAL MIXED CUT

pink color variety

set in gold and worn around the neck, topaz is reputed to dispel bad omens, heal poor vision, and calm anger

OVAL STEP CUT

characteristic wedge-shaped ends

TRANSPARENT SHERRY-COLORED CRYSTAL

TOPAZ RING
A salmon pink, step-cut, eight-sided topaz, set in a gold ring.

FLOWER BROOCH
The heart of this flower-shaped brooch is a round, brilliant-cut topaz, surrounded by 36 sherry-colored topaz gems – some triangular, some diamond-shaped.

SG 3.54	RI 1.62–1.63	DR 0.010	Luster Vitreous

very pale grayish green color •

stones are typically transparent •

ELONGATED OVAL MIXED CUT

• *21,005-carat stone, once the largest gem ever faceted*

SQUARE CUSHION CUT ("THE BRAZILIAN PRINCESS")

blue topaz is also popular •

pale green topaz crystal •

• *blue topaz may be produced by heat treating colorless stones*

TOPAZ CRYSTAL IN MATRIX

• *pegmatite rock*

OCTAGONAL STEP CUT

characteristic tear-shaped inclusions •

stone is partially cut before being heat treated to turn it blue •

Brilliant

Cushion

Pendeloque

Step

Step

Mixed

PENDELOQUE CUT

COLORLESS, PARTIALLY FACETED PEBBLE

Crystal structure Orthorhombic	Composition Beryllium aluminum oxide	Hardness 8½

CHRYSOBERYL

Chrysoberyl occurs in a range of colors, from green, greenish yellow, and yellow to brown. It is a hard, durable stone, particularly suitable for use in jewelry. When cut well, gems are brilliant but lack fire. Two varieties, alexandrite and cat's-eye, have unique qualities of their own. The very rare and valuable alexandrite changes from green in daylight to red, mauve, or brown under incandescent light. Synthetic chrysoberyl, synthetic corundum, and synthetic spinel have all been produced to imitate alexandrite's color change. Cat's-eye, when cut *en cabochon*, has a near-white line across a yellowish gray stone, due to canal- or featherlike fluid inclusions, or needlelike inclusions of rutile. The most highly prized cat's-eye color is a light golden brown, often with a shadow that gives a light and dark, "milk and honey" effect. Yellow chrysoberyl, popular in Portuguese jewelry of the 18th and 19th centuries, was also known as chrysolite.
• **OCCURRENCE** Although most has been mined out, the best chrysoberyl, including alexandrite, has been found in mica schists in the Urals (Russia). The largest faceted chrysoberyl from Russia weighs 66 carats. Large waterworn pebbles of various colors are found in the gem gravels of Sri Lanka. Chrysoberyl also occurs in Myanmar, Brazil, Zimbabwe, Tanzania, and Madagascar. Cat's-eye is found in Sri Lanka, Brazil, and China.
• **REMARK** The name chrysoberyl is from the Greek *chrysos*, meaning golden, and *beryllos*, which refers to the beryllium content. Known for thousands of years in Asia, it was highly valued for the protection it afforded from the "evil eye."

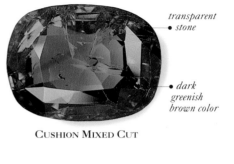

transparent stone

dark greenish brown color

CUSHION MIXED CUT

golden brown color is highly prized

cut stones are brilliant but may lack fire

CUSHION MIXED CUT

greenish yellow cabochon shows faint cat's-eye

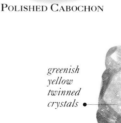

cat's-eye chrysoberyl has also been known as cymophane

POLISHED CABOCHON

FINGER RING
This very large ring, made of many cushion-cut chrysoberyl stones in a gold setting, is most probably of 18th-century Spanish origin. The chrysoberyl was collected from a vein running through chalk.

typical wedge-shaped ends

greenish yellow twinned crystals

SPRAY OF CHRYSOBERYL CRYSTALS

SG 3.71	RI 1.74–1.75	DR 0.009	Luster Vitreous

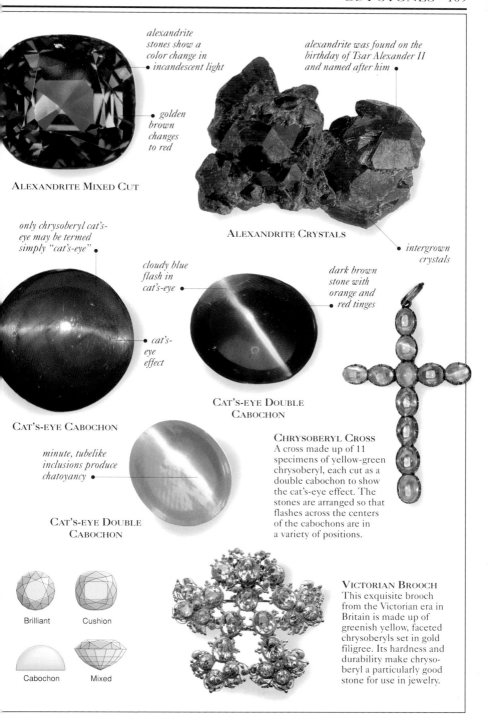

ALEXANDRITE MIXED CUT

alexandrite stones show a color change in incandescent light

golden brown changes to red

alexandrite was found on the birthday of Tsar Alexander II and named after him

ALEXANDRITE CRYSTALS

intergrown crystals

only chrysoberyl cat's-eye may be termed simply "cat's-eye"

cloudy blue flash in cat's-eye

dark brown stone with orange and red tinges

cat's-eye effect

CAT'S-EYE CABOCHON

CAT'S-EYE DOUBLE CABOCHON

minute, tubelike inclusions produce chatoyancy

CAT'S-EYE DOUBLE CABOCHON

CHRYSOBERYL CROSS
A cross made up of 11 specimens of yellow-green chrysoberyl, each cut as a double cabochon to show the cat's-eye effect. The stones are arranged so that flashes across the centers of the cabochons are in a variety of positions.

Brilliant

Cushion

Cabochon

Mixed

VICTORIAN BROOCH
This exquisite brooch from the Victorian era in Britain is made up of greenish yellow, faceted chrysoberyls set in gold filigree. Its hardness and durability make chryso-beryl a particularly good stone for use in jewelry.

Crystal structure Orthorhombic	Composition Aluminum silicate	Hardness 7½

ANDALUSITE

Andalusite varies in color from a pale yellowish brown to a dark bottle green, dark brown, or the most popular greenish red. It has strong and distinctive pleochroism, so that, when turned, the same stone may appear yellow, green, and red. Large crystals may be vertically striated prisms with a square cross section and pyramidal ends, but these are rare. More usual are opaque, rodlike aggregates of crystals or waterworn pebbles. It is the pebbles that are usually cut as gemstones.

• OCCURRENCE Andalusite is usually found in pegmatites. Pebbles occur in the gem gravels of Sri Lanka and Brazil. Other localities include Spain, Canada, Russia, Australia, and the USA.

• REMARK An opaque, yellowish gray variety, chiastolite, occurs as long prisms, which make a cross when cut and polished.

• *pleochroism creates flashes of yellow, green, and red*

OCTAGONAL STEP CUT

"cross" once used as religious • symbol

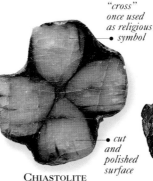

opaque crystals with rhombic • cross section

• *cut and polished surface*

CHIASTOLITE CROSS SECTION

ANDALUSITE CRYSTALS IN MATRIX

Brilliant   Baguette

SG 3.16	RI 1.63–1.64	DR 0.010	Luster Vitreous

Crystal structure Orthorhombic	Composition Calcium borosilicate	Hardness 7

DANBURITE

Generally colorless, danburite crystals may also be yellow or pink. They form wedge-shaped prisms, similar to those of colorless topaz but may be distinguished by their cleavage (poor in danburite, perfect in topaz) and specific gravity (lower in danburite).

• OCCURRENCE First found in the town of Danbury, Connecticut. Gemquality crystals occur in Myanmar, Mexico, Switzerland, Italy, and Japan.

stone from Myanmar has slight yellowish tinge •

stones are bright but • lack fire

characteristic wedge-shaped • end

BRILLIANT CUT

WHITE DANBURITE CRYSTALS

Brilliant   Step   Mixed

SG 3.00	RI 1.63–1.64	DR 0.006	Luster Vitreous to greasy

Crystal structure Orthorhombic	Composition Magnesium iron silicate	Hardness 5½

ENSTATITE

Enstatite is one of the pyroxene family – a series of magnesium- to iron-rich silicates. Crystals occur as short prisms, but are rare: most gem-quality material is faceted from rolled pebbles. Cuttable enstatite varies in color from a gray- to yellowish green or olive green, to an iron-rich brownish green. A brilliant emerald green variety, colored by chromium, also occurs.

• OCCURRENCE Enstatite is often found with kimberlites in South Africa. Brownish green enstatite is found in Myanmar, Norway, and the USA (California). Some Sri Lankan and Indian enstatite is chatoyant. It also occurs in the USA, Switzerland, Greenland, Scotland, Japan, and the former USSR.

double cabochon cut shows cat's-eye effect •

CAT'S-EYE CABOCHON

• clear, yellowish green stone from South Africa

OVAL MIXED CUT

uneven fracture •

massive, fibrous material •

ENSTATITE ROUGH

Step   Cabochon

SG 3.27	RI 1.66–1.67	DR 0.010	Luster Vitreous

Crystal structure Orthorhombic	Composition Aluminum silicate	Hardness 7½

SILLIMANITE

Sillimanite (named after Professor Silliman of Yale University) is blue to green with distinct pleochroism showing pale yellowish green, dark green, and blue from different angles. When crystals occur in long slender prisms in parallel groups, resembling fibers, the material is often called fibrolite.

• OCCURRENCE Sillimanite is found in metamorphic rocks and occasionally in pegmatites. Blue and violet stones are found in Myanmar; greenish gray stones in Sri Lanka; fibrolite in the USA (Idaho). Other sites are Czechoslovakia, India, Italy, Germany, and Brazil.

• pale violet stone from Myanmar

• scissors-cut crown facets

long, slender • crystals

perpendicular fibers • CUSHION MIXED CUT

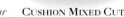

Cushion   Cabochon

FIBROLITE CABOCHON

SILLIMANITE CRYSTALS IN MATRIX

SG 3.25	RI 1.66–1.68	DR 0.019	Luster Vitreous

Crystal structure Orthorhombic	Composition Iron magnesium silicate	Hardness 5½

HYPERSTHENE

Hypersthene is an iron-rich pyroxene in the same series of minerals as enstatite (see p.111) and bronzite. It is distinguished by its reddish iridescence, which is due to platy inclusions of goethite and hematite. Often too dark to facet, it may be cut *en cabochon* instead to show the sparkling inclusions. Bronzite, a greenish brown variety with a bronzelike luster, is also a collector's stone – dark, slightly brittle, and not generally used in jewelry.
• OCCURRENCE Most gem hypersthene is found in India, Norway, Greenland, Germany, and the USA. Bronzite is found in Austria.

colors range from green to grayish black and brown

RECTANGULAR STEP CUT

opaque crystal fragment

 brassy effect

platy inclusions visible

Cushion

Baguette

POLISHED BRONZITE

HYPERSTHENE ROUGH

SG 3.35	RI 1.65–1.67	DR 0.010	Luster Vitreous

Crystal structure Orthorhombic	Composition Magnesium aluminum silicate	Hardness 7

IOLITE

Violet-blue iolite (also known as cordierite) has been called water sapphire because of its similarity to blue sapphire when cut. It can be recognized by its strong pleochroism, visible without equipment, which gives the gem its other name of dichroite. The best blue color is seen down the length of prismatic crystals; they may appear colorless when viewed across.
• OCCURRENCE Gem-quality iolite is found in alluvial deposits as small, transparent, waterworn pebbles in Sri Lanka, Myanmar, Madagascar, and India. Other localities include Namibia and Tanzania. Crystals are found in Germany, Norway, and Finland.

rich violet-blue tinge

more intense color visible from front

paler color visible from this angle

IOLITE CUBE – VIEW 1

purplish blue crystal

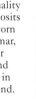

IOLITE CUBE – VIEW 2

CRYSTAL IN MATRIX

Step

Cabochon

Mixed

SG 2.63	RI 1.53–1.55	DR 0.010	Luster Vitreous

Crystal structure Orthorhombic	Composition Magnesium aluminum borosilicate	Hardness 6½

KORNERUPINE

Although kornerupine was named in 1884, it was not until 1912 that gem-quality material was found. Even now it is uncommon and cut only for collectors. Strongly pleochroic, it appears green or reddish brown when viewed from different directions. To show the best color, it is cut with the table facet parallel to the length of the crystal.
• OCCURRENCE Localities include Madagascar, Sri Lanka, and East Africa, which also produces an emerald green variety. Cat's-eye gems are cut from Sri Lankan and East African stones.
• REMARK It has been confused with tourmaline and enstatite.

distinctive grayish green color

RECTANGULAR STEP CUT

• *kornerupine gems are rare and prized by collectors*

dark kornerupine crystals

MIXED CUT

CRYSTALS IN MATRIX

Cushion   Baguette   Step

SG 3.32	RI 1.66–1.68	DR 0.013	Luster Vitreous

Crystal structure Orthorhombic	Composition Magnesium iron silicate	Hardness 6½

PERIDOT

Gem-quality specimens of the mineral olivine are called peridot by gemologists. Peridot has an olive- or bottle green color that is due to the presence of iron, and a distinctive oily or greasy luster. It has a high birefraction, so doubling of the back facets can easily be seen in larger specimens when viewed from the front. Good-quality crystals are very rare.
• OCCURRENCE Sources of peridot include St. John's Island (Egypt), China, Myanmar, Brazil, Norway, the USA (Arizona and Hawaii), Australia, and South Africa.
• REMARK The Crusaders brought peridot to Europe in the Middle Ages from St. John's Island in the Red Sea, where it had been mined for over 3,500 years.

• *green color due to iron*

distinctive bottle green color

OVAL MIXED CUT

peridot was often used in religious jewelry

OCTAGONAL MIXED CUT

CRYSTAL FRAGMENT

Pendeloque   Step   Cabochon

SG 3.34	RI 1.64–1.69	DR 0.036	Luster Vitreous to greasy

Crystal structure Orthorhombic	Composition Lead sulfate		Hardness 3

ANGLESITE

Anglesite is usually colorless or with a slight yellowish tinge but may also be found as gray, green, purple, brown, or black crystals (the black coloring is due to inclusions of galena). Crystals are heavy but as they are fragile and soft, with perfect cleavage, they are faceted for collectors only.

• **OCCURRENCE** Anglesite is formed by oxidation of galena (lead sulfide) and may be found in Anglesey in Wales (hence the name) and in the Leadhills district of Scotland. The best crystals are found in Tsumeb (Namibia) and Morocco. Other localities include Germany, the USA, and Sardinia.

• stones often have a slight yellowish tinge

transparent anglesite crystal with pointed end •

galena matrix

FANCY CUT

Step

ANGLESITE CRYSTALS IN MATRIX

SG 6.35	RI 1.87–1.89	DR 0.017	Luster Waxy to adamantine

Crystal structure Orthorhombic	Composition Magnesium aluminum iron borate		Hardness 6½

SINHALITE

Until 1952, sinhalite was thought to be a brown variety of peridot, but on closer investigation it was found to be a completely new mineral. It varies from a pale yellowish brown to a dark greenish brown. Crystals have distinct pleochroism, showing pale brown, greenish brown, and dark brown when viewed from different directions. Occasionally, sinhalite has been faceted for the collector. Cut stones may be confused with peridot, chrysoberyl, and zircon.

• **OCCURRENCE** Most gem-quality sinhalite is found as rolled pebbles in the gem gravels of Sri Lanka. Crystals occur in Myanmar but are rare. Sinhalite is also found in the former USSR, and non-gem-quality material in the USA.

• **REMARK** Sinhalite is named after *sinhala*, which is the Sanskrit name for Sri Lanka.

pale yellowish • brown stone

• cut is slightly irregular to conserve weight

CUSHION MIXED CUT

double-ended, waterworn • prism

dark yellow- • brown

Step   Mixed

CUSHION MIXED CUT

SINHALITE CRYSTAL

SG 3.48	RI 1.67–1.71	DR 0.038	Luster Vitreous

Crystal structure Orthorhombic	Composition Beryllium hydroxyborate	Hardness 7½

HAMBERGITE

Hambergite, named after Axel Hamberg, the Swedish mineralogist, occurs as colorless to yellowish white crystals, but it is rare at gem quality. Brittle, with perfect cleavage, it is very fragile and suitable only for collectors. When cut, it looks like glass, but double images of the back facets may be seen through the table facet due to its high birefraction.

• OCCURRENCE Gem-quality hambergite is found in Kashmir (India), and also in Madagascar.

transparent stones for faceting are rare

OVAL MIXED CUT

surface coloring from host rock

deep striations along length

brown mineral inclusions

OVAL MIXED CUT

HAMBERGITE CRYSTAL

Brilliant   Step

SG 2.35	RI 1.55–1.63	DR 0.072	Luster Vitreous

Crystal structure Orthorhombic	Composition Calcium aluminum hydroxysilicate	Hardness 6

PREHNITE

Often an oily green, prehnite may also range from pale yellowish to brown. Columnar or tabular crystals are rare: it occurs more usually as aggregates of barrel-shaped crystals or as botryoidal masses. Some pale yellowish brown prehnite is fibrous enough to be cut *en cabochon* and may show the cat's-eye effect.

• OCCURRENCE Prehnite is found in basaltic volcanic rocks, in intrusive igneous rocks, and in some metamorphic rocks. Pale green masses are found in Scotland; dark green or greenish brown masses in Australia; aggregates of crystals in France.

• REMARK Prehnite is named after Colonel von Prehn, who first introduced prehnite to Europe.

stones are generally translucent

BRILLIANT-CUT STONES

faceted gems are usually small

STEP CUT

fractures radiate out from reddish inclusions

translucent crystals in botryoidal masses

POLISHED FRAGMENT

CRYSTALS ON MATRIX

Baguette

Step

Cabochon

SG 2.87	RI 1.61–1.64	DR 0.016	Luster Vitreous

Crystal structure Orthorhombic	Composition Calcium aluminum hydroxysilicate	Hardness 6½

ZOISITE

Zoisite occurs in a number of varieties, the most sought after being tanzanite, a variety colored sapphire blue by the presence of vanadium. Tanzanite crystals have distinct pleochroism, showing either purple, blue, or slate gray, depending on the angle they are viewed from. There may also be a slight color change in incandescent light, when stones may appear more violet. A massive green variety of zoisite, containing rubies and occasionally dark hornblende inclusions, may be polished, carved, or tumbled to make ornaments or an attractive decorative stone. Thulite, a massive, pinkish red variety colored by manganese, is also polished or carved to make small ornaments. Tanzanite has been confused with sapphire, and thulite with rhodonite. Some heating of zoisite varieties may enhance their color.

• OCCURRENCE Tanzanite was first found in Tanzania (hence the name). Yellow and green zoisite occurs in Tanzania and Kenya. Thulite is found in Norway, Austria, western Australia, Italy, and in the USA (North Carolina).

• REMARK Discovered by Baron von Zois in the Sau-Alp mountains of Austria, zoisite was first called saualpite.

stone has been heat treated to enhance color •

• color varies from purple to blue due to pleochroism

TANZANITE MIXED CUT

pale bluish violet • color

stones are • soft and brittle

TANZANITE STEP CUT

• tanzanite has perfect cleavage

violet-blue tanzanite • crystal

TANZANITE CRYSTAL

TANZANITE CRYSTAL IN MATRIX

• polished zoisite is often used for decorative work

pinkish red color • due to manganese

THULITE SLAB

THULITE CABOCHON

massive habit •

intergrown grayish white quartz •

Step

Cabochon

Cameo

THULITE ROUGH

SG 3.35	RI 1.69–1.70	DR 0.010	Luster Vitreous

Crystal structure Orthorhombic	Composition Aluminum iron hydroxysilicate	Hardness 7

STAUROLITE

Opaque, cross-shaped staurolite "twins" are used in jewelry more often than the transparent stones, which are rare and cut only for collectors. "Cross stones," as twins are called, have been used as amulets and in religious jewelry. Crystals are reddish brown to black, with distinct pleochroism.
• OCCURRENCE Staurolite occurs in Switzerland, Germany, the former USSR, the USA, Brazil, France, and Scotland.

cross shape formed by
• twinned crystals

short, black
staurolite
• crystals

opaque
• stone

CROSS STONE

CRYSTALS
IN MATRIX

Baguette	Step	Cameo

SG 3.72	RI 1.74–1.75	DR 0.013	Luster Vitreous

Crystal structure Orthorhombic	Composition Aluminum iron borosilicate	Hardness 7

DUMORTIERITE

Dumortierite is best known in its massive form, which makes an attractive violet and blue decorative stone when polished. Reddish brown and red varieties also occur. Prismatic crystals larger than ½₅ in (1 mm) are very rare. Dumortierite is also found intergrown with rock crystal (colorless quartz) and is then called dumortierite quartz. This material is usually cut *en cabochon* or polished to make decorative stones.
• OCCURRENCE Most gem-quality material is found in Nevada. Other localities include France, Madagascar, Norway, Sri Lanka, Canada, Poland, Namibia, and Italy.
• REMARK Dumortierite was named after the French scientist M.E. Dumortier.

surface may
become pitted
• when polished

DUMORTIERITE
QUARTZ CABOCHON

distinctive deep
blue color •

CARVED BOTTLE
Hard but attractive, dumortierite is often polished and carved to make decorative objects, like this bottle adorned with the image of a bird.

DUMORTIERITE
QUARTZ SLAB

splintery
surface •

MASSIVE
DUMORTIERITE

Cabochon	Cameo	Polished

SG 3.28	RI 1.69–1.72	DR 0.037	Luster Vitreous

Crystal structure Monoclinic	Composition Sodium beryllium phosphate	Hardness 5½

BERYLLONITE

Beryllonite crystals are colorless, white, or pale yellow, but its weak fire and low dispersion make it a dull gemstone. In addition, its softness, perfect cleavage, and brittle fracture make it fragile, although with care it may be faceted for collectors.
• OCCURRENCE Beryllonite is a pegmatite mineral found associated with the minerals phenakite and berylin in Maine. It is also found in Finland and Zimbabwe but remains a rare gem.
• REMARK Beryllonite is named after the beryllium content in its chemical composition. It has been confused with other colorless gemstones of low dispersion.

crystals are usually colorless

weak fire and low dispersion mean gems appear dull

CUSHION MIXED CUT

cleavage planes visible

stones are soft and easily damaged

CUSHION MIXED CUT

BERYLLONITE CRYSTAL

Brilliant   Cushion   Pendeloque

SG 2.83	RI 1.55–1.56	DR 0.009	Luster Vitreous

Crystal structure Monoclinic	Composition Aluminum sodium hydroxyphosphate	Hardness 5½

BRAZILIANITE

Brazilianite is a rare and unusual gemstone. Cut for collectors only, its yellow or yellowish green color is nonetheless striking. Crystals are fragile and brittle, with conchoidal fracture and perfect cleavage perpendicular to their length.
• OCCURRENCE The main localities are in Brazil, where crystals up to 6 in (15 cm) have been found. Smaller crystals have been mined in New Hampshire.
• REMARK Found in Minas Gerais in Brazil in 1944, brazilianite was first thought to be chrysoberyl, but closer examination revealed it to be a completely new mineral. It was named after the country in which it was found but has since been confused with chrysoberyl, beryl, and topaz.

distinctive greenish yellow color

RECTANGULAR STEP CUT

stones chip and flaw easily

apatite crystals

yellow brazilianite crystals

STEP CUT

GROUP OF CRYSTALS

Cushion   Pendeloque   Baguette

SG 2.99	RI 1.60–1.62	DR 0.021	Luster Vitreous

Crystal structure Monoclinic	Composition Calcium magnesium silicate	Hardness 5½

DIOPSIDE

Crystals of diopside may be colorless but are more usually bottle green, brownish green, or light green. The more iron-rich and magnesium-poor they are, the darker the color – almost to black. Very bright green diopside, colored by chromium, is known as chrome diopside. Violet-blue crystals, colored by manganese, have been found in Italy and the USA, and may be called violane. It is polished as beads when massive, cut for collectors when transparent, and cut *en cabochon* when fibrous.
• OCCURRENCE Gem-quality chrome diopside is found in Myanmar, Siberia (Russia), Pakistan, and South Africa. Other diopside localities include Austria, Brazil, Italy, the USA, Madagascar, Canada, and Sri Lanka. Dark green to black diopside, which shows a 4-rayed star when cut *en cabochon*, has been found in southern India since 1964.

flaws are due to diopside's fragility

chrome diopside variety is bright emerald green

OCTAGONAL STEP CUT

RECTANGULAR STEP CUT

dark green diopside crystals

DIOPSIDE IN MATRIX

Brilliant Baguette Step Cabochon

SG 3.29	RI 1.66–1.72	DR 0.029	Luster Vitreous

Crystal structure Monoclinic	Composition Hydrated magnesium silicate	Hardness 2½

MEERSCHAUM

Meerschaum, also known as sepiolite, is a very fine-grained, soft, light rock. Found as compact, opaque masses with an earthy or chalky appearance, it may be white or gray with a yellowish or reddish tinge. Easily fashioned and often intricately carved, meerschaum is still used in Turkey for pipe bowls. With use, the smoke changes the white stone to an attractive yellow color.
• OCCURRENCE Today the most important source is Eskischehir in Turkey. Other localities include Czechoslovakia, Spain, Greece, and the USA.
• REMARK Light and porous enough to float on water, meerschaum derives its name from the German for "sea foam."

BEAD NECKLACE Soft and light, meerschaum is easy to carve into intricate objects, such as the individually worked beads on this delicate Turkish necklace.

dull, earthy luster

light, porous, creamy white meerschaum

MASSIVE ROUGH

Bead Cameo

SG 1.50	RI 1.51–1.53	DR None	Luster Dull to greasy

Crystal structure Monoclinic	Composition Lithium aluminum silicate	Hardness 7

SPODUMENE

Spodumene occurs in a range of colors, although the most common variety is yellowish gray. Two gem varieties – lilac-pink kunzite (colored by manganese) and bright emerald green hiddenite (colored by chromium) – are popular with collectors, although perfect cleavage makes them fragile gemstones. Strong pleochroism is easily seen in gem material, showing colorless and two shades of the body color when viewed from different directions. Stones should always be cut to show the best color through the table facet. The pink color may fade with time, but some material is irradiated to intensify it.

• **OCCURRENCE** Spodumene was discovered in 1877 in Brazil, although it was not until 1879 that kunzite and hiddenite were recognized as different varieties of the same mineral. Spodumene is also found in Madagascar, Myanmar, the USA, Canada, the former USSR, Mexico, and Sweden.

• **REMARK** Lilac-pink kunzite is named after the gemologist G.F. Kunz, who first described it in 1902; hiddenite is named after W.E. Hidden, who discovered it in North Carolina in 1879.

lilac-pink color due to manganese

characteristic striations parallel to length

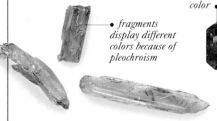

CUSHION-CUT KUNZITE

very pale green color

OCTAGONAL STEP CUT

KUNZITE CRYSTAL

fragments display different colors because of pleochroism

emerald green color

closeup of hiddenite crystals

STEP-CUT HIDDENITE

HIDDENITE CRYSTAL FRAGMENTS

gneiss matrix

HIDDENITE CRYSTALS IN MATRIX

Brilliant   Pendeloque   Step   Step

SG 3.18	RI 1.66–1.67	DR 0.015	Luster Vitreous

Crystal structure Monoclinic	Composition Calcium aluminum iron hydroxysilicate	Hardness 6½

EPIDOTE

This fairly dense, fragile mineral has distinct cleavage and is rarely cut as a gemstone. Crystals are yellow, green, or dark brown columnar prisms, with faces finely striated parallel to the crystal's length. Pleochroism is strong, showing either yellow, green, or brown. Rock made up mainly of epidote may be polished or tumbled and sold as "unakite."

• OCCURRENCE Dark green crystals occur in the Austrian and French Alps. Epidote is also found in the former USSR, Italy, the island of Elba (Italy), Mozambique, and Mexico.

• *stones are fragile and easily flawed*

dark brown color •

MIXED CUT

columnar epidote crystals •

parallel striations •

RECTANGULAR TABLE CUT

EPIDOTE CRYSTALS IN MATRIX

Cushion

Step

SG 3.40	RI 1.74–1.78	DR 0.035	Luster Vitreous

Crystal structure Monoclinic	Composition Calcium titanium silicate	Hardness 5

TITANITE

Titanite, also known as sphene, is known for its very strong fire (its dispersion is higher than that of diamond) and rich colors, but it is seldom used in jewelry because it is too brittle and soft. Nevertheless, transparent yellow, green, or brown gem-quality material is cut for collectors. Titanite is strongly pleochroic (showing three different colors) and has high birefraction (seen as doubling of the back facets) and adamantine luster.

• OCCURRENCE Gem-quality titanite occurs in cavities in metamorphic rocks such as gneiss and schist and also in granite. Locations include Austria, Canada, Switzerland, Madagascar, Mexico, and Brazil.

doubling of back facets due to high birefraction •

• *high dispersion gives facets of varying colors*

CUSHION MIXED CUT

characteristic wedge-shaped ends •

twinned titanite crystals •

TITANITE RING
Faceted stones, like this bright yellow brilliant cut set in gold, have high fire and rich colors.

Brilliant   Baguette   Mixed

TITANITE CRYSTALS IN MATRIX

SG 3.53	RI 1.84–2.03	DR 0.120	Luster Adamantine

Crystal structure Monoclinic	Composition Potassium aluminum silicate	Hardness 6

COLORLESS ORTHOCLASE

Orthoclase, an alkali feldspar, occurs in a range of colors, the most common being colorless. Adularia, a colorless, transparent variety from Adular-Bergstock in Switzerland, has a bluish white "schiller," or sheen, called adularescence.

• OCCURRENCE Orthoclase feldspar occurs in intrusive igneous rocks and is one of the main constituents of granitic pegmatites. It is also found in metamorphic rocks such as schist and gneiss. Clear, colorless orthoclase occurs in Madagascar. Yellow and colorless cuttable material, cat's-eyes, and some star stones occur in the gem gravels of Sri Lanka and Myanmar.

• REMARK Feldspars are the most common rock-forming minerals at the Earth's surface. They are divided into two groups, the alkali feldspars and the plagioclase feldspars (see p.130). Orthoclase derives its name from the Greek for "break straight," a reference to its perfect cleavage at near 90 degrees.

colorless, transparent stone •

ADULARIA CUSHION CUT

internal cracks • or flaws

white orthoclase crystals •

Brilliant

Mixed

ADULARIA CRYSTAL

ORTHOCLASE WITH QUARTZ

SG 2.56	RI 1.51–1.54	DR 0.005	Luster Vitreous

Crystal structure Monoclinic	Composition Potassium aluminum silicate	Hardness 6

YELLOW ORTHOCLASE

The yellow variety of orthoclase feldspar (see colorless orthoclase above) is usually faceted as a step cut because the stones are often fragile. The yellow color is due to the presence of iron. Orthoclase crystals are columnar or tabular prisms, and are often twinned.

• OCCURRENCE The best yellow orthoclase is found in Madagascar in pegmatites, and may be faceted for the collector. Yellow orthoclase from Madagascar and Germany may be cut *en cabochon* to show the cat's-eye effect.

• REMARK Feldspars form in igneous and metamorphic rocks. Which type is formed depends on the temperature it forms at and how it cools.

• step cut is most common, because of fragility of stone

crystals may be translucent to semitranslucent •

Step

RECTANGULAR STEP CUT

CRYSTAL FRAGMENT

SG 2.56	RI 1.51–1.54	DR 0.005	Luster Vitreous

Crystal structure Monoclinic	Composition Potassium aluminum silicate	Hardness 6

MOONSTONE (ORTHOCLASE)

Moonstone is the opalescent variety of orthoclase, with a blue or white sheen (or "schiller"), rather like the shine of the moon. This is caused by the reflection of light from the internal structure, made up of alternating layers of albite and orthoclase feldspar. Thin albite layers give an attractive blue; while thicker layers produce a white "schiller." Stones of large size and fine quality are rare.

• OCCURRENCE The best material is from Myanmar and Sri Lanka. Other localities include India, Madagascar, Brazil, the USA, Mexico, Tanzania, and the European Alps.

milky opalescence on table facet

CUSHION BRILLIANT CUT

pitted surface has frosted glass appearance

BLUE MOON
The moonstone in this finely detailed cameo has a distinct blue "schiller." Moon worshippers through the ages have used it in their jewelry.

WATERWORN PEBBLE

| Cushion | Cabochon | Cameo |

| SG 2.57 | RI 1.52–1.53 | DR 0.005 | Luster Vitreous |

Crystal structure Triclinic	Composition Potassium aluminum silicate	Hardness 6

MICROCLINE

A form of alkali feldspar, microcline may be colorless, white, yellow, pink, red, gray, green, or blue-green. However, the semi-opaque, blue-green variety called amazonite (named after the Amazon River) is most commonly used in jewelry, and may be cut, usually *en cabochon*, up to almost any size. Its striking color is due to the presence of lead.

• OCCURRENCE The most important source of amazonite is India. Other localities include the USA, Canada, the former USSR, Madagascar, Tanzania, and Namibia.

• REMARK Although microcline has the same composition as orthoclase, its crystal structure is triclinic.

characteristic blue-green color

amazonite may be confused with jade or turquoise

some surfaces have silky luster

AMAZONITE CABOCHON

polished surface shows cleavage planes

blue, massive material

AMAZONITE SLAB

AMAZONITE ROUGH

| Bead | Cabochon | Cameo |

| SG 2.56 | RI 1.52–1.53 | DR 0.008 | Luster Vitreous to silky |

Crystal structure Monoclinic	Composition Sodium aluminum silicate	Hardness 7

JADEITE (JADE)

For centuries, jade was thought to be a single gemstone, but in 1863 two types were recognized: jadeite and nephrite. Nephrite (opposite) is more common, but both are tough, fine-grained rocks, suitable for carving. Jadeite, made up of interlocking, granular pyroxene crystals, occurs in a wide range of colors including green, lilac, white, pink, brown, red, blue, black, orange, and yellow. The most prized variety, imperial jade, is a rich emerald green, due to chromium. Jadeite commonly has a dimpled surface when polished.

• OCCURRENCE Jadeite is found in metamorphic rocks and as alluvial pebbles or boulders. Some boulders develop a brown skin from weathering, and this is often incorporated into carvings and worked pieces. The most important source of jade is Myanmar, which has supplied China with translucent imperial jade for over 200 years. Historically, Guatemala was an important source of jade, providing the material for the carvings of the Central American Indians. Jadeite also occurs in Japan and the USA (California).

• REMARK The Spanish *conquistadores* adopted the use of jadeite when they invaded Central America, and often wore amulets made from it. They called it *piedra de hijada* (loin stone) or *piedra de los rinones* (kidney stone), believing it prevented or cured hip and kidney complaints.

black inclusions •

characteristic emerald green • color

POLISHED IMPERIAL JADE

MEXICAN MASK
This opaque, mottled green mask was carved in Mexico, probably before 1753. Older jadeite carvings have a characteristic pitted surface; modern abrasives give a smoother finish.

massive habit •

mottled jadeite, fashioned and • polished

violet color caused by traces of iron •

JADEITE SPHERE

Bead

Cameo

Polished

POLISHED SLAB

SG 3.33	RI 1.66–1.68	DR 0.012	Luster Greasy to pearly

Crystal structure Monoclinic	Composition Calcium magnesium iron silicate	Hardness 6½

NEPHRITE (JADE)

Nephrite, recognized as a separate type of jade since 1863 (see opposite), is found as aggregates of fibrous amphibole crystals. These form an interlocking structure tougher than steel, hence nephrite's popularity as a material for carving – first for weapons and later for ornaments. Colors vary from a dark green, iron-rich nephrite to a cream-colored, magnesium-rich variety. Nephrite jade may be homogeneous in color, blotchy, or banded.

• OCCURRENCE Nephrite jade has been carved by the Chinese for over 2,000 years, though the raw material was probably first imported from Turkestan, Central Asia, and later from Myanmar. Other localities include Siberia (dark green rocks, often with black spots), Russia (spinach-colored stones), and China. Nephrite jade is also found in various rocks in the North and South Islands of New Zealand (pieces carved in the 17th century include Maori clubs called *meres*). Other localities include Australia (black nephrite), the USA, Canada, Mexico, Brazil, Taiwan, Zimbabwe (dark green), Italy, Poland, Germany, and Switzerland.

• REMARK Nephrite may be confused with bowenite serpentine; it may be imitated by composite stones or dyed to improve color.

CHINESE CARVING
Nephrite jade has been carved in China for centuries and is tough enough to be worked into intricate designs. China is still one of the world's main jade-cutting centers.

DAGGER HANDLE
Because of its great strength, nephrite has been used since prehistoric times to make weapons. In fact, at one time it was known as "ax stone."

color may • be blotchy

FABERGÉ SNAIL
The greasy luster of nephrite jade enhances this witty carving by the famous Russian jeweler, Fabergé.

CHINESE CAMEL
The shape of the original boulder has been integrated into the design of this carving. Only one side of the boulder has been fashioned.

tough, interlocking structure •

Bead

Cameo

Polished

NEPHRITE BOULDER

SG 2.96	RI 1.61–1.63	DR 0.027	Luster Greasy to pearly

Crystal structure Monoclinic	Composition Copper hydroxycarbonate		Hardness 4

MALACHITE

Malachite is usually found in opaque green masses, its color derived from copper. Crystals are too small for faceting, but the massive material is carved or polished in many ways to reveal the alternating bands of light and dark green. In the past, malachite was worn to ward off danger and illness.
• OCCURRENCE Malachite occurs in small quantities worldwide and in larger quantities in copper-mining areas. Zaire is the most important producer.

• *concentric green to near-black banding*

common botryoidal habit

POLISHED MALACHITE

Cabochon

MALACHITE ROUGH

SG 3.80	RI 1.85 (mean)	DR 0.025	Luster Vitreous to silky

Crystal structure Monoclinic	Composition Hydrated copper silicate		Hardness 2

CHRYSOCOLLA

Chrysocolla usually occurs as a bright green or bluish crust, or as compact, grapelike groups. Crystals intergrown with quartz or with opal are more commonly used in jewelry.
• OCCURRENCE Copper-mining areas, particularly Chile, the former USSR, and Zaire. "Eilat Stone" (intergrown with malachite and turquoise) reputedly came from King Solomon's mines.

Bead

• *brown patches of copper ore*

crystals are very small (microcrystalline)

POLISHED CHRYSOCOLLA

CHRYSOCOLLA ROUGH

SG 2.20	RI 1.57–1.63	DR 0.030	Luster Greasy to vitreous

Crystal structure Monoclinic	Composition Copper hydroxycarbonate		Hardness 3½

AZURITE

Azurite is an azure blue copper mineral, occasionally found as prismatic crystals (rarely faceted), but more usually in massive form intergrown with malachite.
• OCCURRENCE Found particularly in copper-mining areas such as Australia, Chile, the former USSR, Africa, and China. Stones from Chessy, near Lyons in France, are called chessylite.

Cameo

• *bands of green malachite*

dark blue azurite crystals

• *polished stone*

BANDED CHESSYLITE

AZURITE CRYSTALS ON MATRIX

• *green malachite*

SG 3.77	RI 1.73–1.84	DR 0.110	Luster Vitreous

Crystal structure Monoclinic	Composition Magnesium hydroxysilicate	Hardness 5

SERPENTINE

The name serpentine refers to a group of predominantly green minerals that occur in masses of tiny intergrown crystals. The two main types used in jewelry are bowenite (translucent green or blue-green) and the rarer williamsite (translucent, oily green, veined or spotted with inclusions). They may be carved, engraved, or polished. Various marbles also contain serpentine veins.

• **OCCURRENCE** Bowenite is found in New Zealand, China, Afghanistan, South Africa, and the USA; Williamsite occurs in Italy, England, and China.

characteristic patches formed
• *by inclusions*

• *partly translucent*

rock composed of various serpentine
• *minerals*

WILLIAMSITE CABOCHON

• *lack of color due to thinness of slice*

Cameo   Polished

BOWENITE PENDANT

SERPENTINITE ROCK

SG 2.60	RI 1.55–1.56	DR 0.001	Luster Vitreous to greasy

Crystal structure Monoclinic	Composition Hydrated zinc phosphate	Hardness 3½

PHOSPHOPHYLLITE

This is one of the rarest of gemstones, and is highly prized by collectors. The crystals, which are prismatic or with a thick, tabular habit, range from colorless to deep bluish green, but the best specimens are a very delicate bluish green. Nevertheless, phosphophyllite is rarely cut, as the material is brittle and fragile, and large crystals are too valuable to be broken up.

• **OCCURRENCE** The finest crystals, and the only ones to be faceted, are from Bolivia. Other localities include Germany and the USA (New Hampshire).

pale blue-green color is most
• *sought after*

cuttable material mainly from
• *Bolivia*

RECTANGULAR STEP CUT

small fragments can
• *be faceted*

crystals crack
• *easily*

STEP CUT

phosphophyllite
• *crystals*

Brilliant   Step

PHOSPHOPHYLLITE CRYSTALS

PHOSPHOPHYLLITE CRYSTALS ON PYRITE

SG 3.10	RI 1.59–1.62	DR 0.021	Luster Vitreous

Crystal structure Monoclinic	Composition Magnesium aluminum hydroxyphosphate	Hardness 5½

LAZULITE

Crystals of lazulite are rare. Colors vary from a mottled pale blue to dark blue. Transparent stones are pleochroic, showing blue and colorless, but often lazulite is not transparent. Semi-translucent or opaque stones, found as small crystal fragments, may be polished, carved, or tumbled to make beads or decorative stones.
• **OCCURRENCE** Localities include the USA, Brazil, India, Sweden, Austria, Switzerland, Madagascar, and Angola.

blue and white mottling

bipyramidal lazulite crystal

POLISHED CABOCHON

Cabochon

LAZULITE IN MATRIX

SG 3.10	RI 1.61–1.64	DR 0.031	Luster Vitreous

Crystal structure Monoclinic	Composition Hydrated calcium borosilicate	Hardness 3½

HOWLITE

Howlite is a soft, light mineral with a chalky white color, commonly with black or brown veins. Crystals are occasionally found in groups. It is very porous and may be dyed to imitate other minerals, especially turquoise.
• **OCCURRENCE** Howlite has been found in large quantities in the USA (California).
• **REMARK** Though it is soft, howlite will withstand a polish and is occasionally used as a decorative stone.

stained blue to imitate turquoise

light, powdery, and porous

Bead

vitreous luster

STAINED HOWLITE

MASSIVE ROUGH

SG 2.58	RI 1.58–1.59	DR 0.022	Luster Vitreous

Crystal structure Monoclinic	Composition Hydrated calcium sulfate	Hardness 2

GYPSUM

Several varieties of gypsum are used as decorative stones. The most important, alabaster, is found as fine-grained masses in pastel shades but is commonly stained in stronger colors. Selenite is colorless, occasionally cut for collectors, but is very soft. Satin spar is a fibrous variety, polished or cut *en cabochon*. Rose shapes (called "desert rose") also occur.
• **OCCURRENCE** Localities include Italy and England (alabaster); Italy, Mexico, the USA, and Chile (selenite).

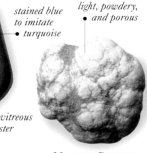

cat's-eye effect

parallel fibrous structure

Cabochon

POLISHED SATIN SPAR

satin luster

SATIN SPAR ROUGH

SG 2.32	RI 1.52–1.53	DR 0.010	Luster Silky to vitreous

Crystal structure Monoclinic	Composition Calcium hydroxyborosilicate		Hardness 5

DATOLITE

Transparent, colorless crystals of datolite are cut for the collector only. A tinge of yellow, green, or white may also be present. More often, however, datolite occurs as a massive material, which may contain copper inclusions.
• **OCCURRENCE** Localites include Austria, Italy, Norway, the USA, Germany, and England. The main source of massive datolite with inclusions is the Lake Superior area of North America.

crystals are cut for collectors only •

colorless, with tinge of yellow •

OCTAGONAL
STEP CUT

Step

CRYSTAL

SG 2.95	RI 1.62–1.65	DR 0.044	Luster Vitreous

Crystal structure Monoclinic	Composition Lithium aluminum silicate		Hardness 6

PETALITE

Fine petalite is rare and fragile. For this reason it is only occasionally cut for the collector. Crystals are transparent, colorless, or white, occurring as tabular or columnar prisms with a glassy appearance. Massive petalite is more common, cut *en cabochon*.
• **OCCURRENCE** Elba (Italy), Brazil, Australia, Sweden, Finland, USA, Zimbabwe, and Namibia.

fine stones are • *rare and fragile*

fibrous, massive material •

CUSHION MIXED CUT

Cushion

PETALITE ROUGH

SG 2.42	RI 1.50–1.51	DR 0.014	Luster Vitreous to pearly

Crystal structure Monoclinic	Composition Beryllium aluminum hydroxysilicate		Hardness 7½

EUCLASE

Euclase is a rare gem. The most attractive color is a pale aquamarine blue, but it also occurs in white, green, and colorless forms. Crystals are prismatic with a perfect cleavage, which means they are fragile and must be cut and handled with care.
• **OCCURRENCE** Euclase occurs mainly in pegmatites. Localities include Brazil, Tanzania, Zaire, Kenya, the former USSR, India, Zimbabwe, and the USA.

black mineral • *inclusions*

striated • *prism*

SQUARE STEP CUT

conchoidal fracture •

Step

PRISMATIC CRYSTAL

SG 3.10	RI 1.65–1.67	DR 0.019	Luster Vitreous

Crystal structure Triclinic	Composition Sodium calcium aluminosilicate	Hardness 6

ALBITE

Albite is one of six species in the plagioclase feldspar series. Each species is
defined by its albite and anorthite content:
albite itself has the highest albite content.
It is usually white, though gems are often
colorless. Peristerite, an albite-oligoclase
mix, has a blue sheen, like moonstone (see p.123).
• OCCURRENCE
The best specimens
of peristerite are
found in Canada.

*albite is
usually
• colorless*

*cream-colored,
• opaque crystals*

Brilliant

Brilliant

MIXED CUT

ALBITE CRYSTALS

SG 2.64	RI 1.54–1.55	DR 0.009	Luster Vitreous to pearly

Crystal structure Triclinic	Composition Sodium calcium aluminosilicate	Hardness 6

OLIGOCLASE

Oligoclase is a species of plagioclase
feldspar (see above). The variety used
in jewelry is called sunstone or, less
commonly, aventurine feldspar. It has
reflective inclusions of red, orange, or
green platy crystals, which give it a
metallic glitter. Sunstone may be faceted or carved, often as cabochons.
• OCCURRENCE Sunstone
occurs in metamorphic and
igneous rocks in Norway,
the USA, India, the former
USSR, and Canada.

SUNSTONE PIN
The bright
spangles in this
cabochon, set
as a tie pin,
are caused by
tiny inclusions
of hematite.

*hematite flakes
produce sparkling
parallel bands •*

Cabochon

SUNSTONE ROUGH

SG 2.64	RI 1.54–1.55	DR 0.007	Luster Vitreous

Crystal structure Triclinic	Composition Sodium calcium aluminosilicate	Hardness 6

LABRADORITE

Labradorite is the plagioclase feldspar (see albite, above) that is most
commonly faceted as a gemstone. It
may be orange, yellow, colorless, or
red, but the material that shows a play
of color, or "schiller," is the most
popular for use in jewelry.
• OCCURRENCE Occurs in
metamorphic and igneous
rocks in Labrador
(Canada), Finland,
Norway, and the
former USSR.

*play of color
(schiller) seen
on polished
• surface*

*interference
of light at
junctions of
internal
• structures*

CABOCHON

Cabochon

Polished

LABRADORITE
ROUGH

SG 2.70	RI 1.56–1.57	DR 0.010	Luster Vitreous

Crystal structure Triclinic	Composition Hydrated copper aluminum phosphate	Hardness 6

TURQUOISE

One of the first gemstones to be mined, turquoise has long been prized for its intense color, which varies from sky blue to green, depending on the quantities of iron and copper within it. Turquoise is commonly found in microcrystalline, massive form, usually as encrustations, in veins, or as nodules. It is opaque to semitranslucent, light and very fragile, with conchoidal fracture. Some material is very porous, leading to fading and cracking, so it may be impregnated with wax or resin to maintain its appearance.

• **OCCURRENCE** Sky blue turquoise from Iran is generally regarded as the most desirable, but in Tibet a greener variety is preferred. Localities in Mexico and the USA produce a greener, more porous material that tends to fade more quickly. Other localities include the former USSR, Chile, Australia, Turkestan, and Cornwall (England).

• **REMARK** Turquoise has been thought to warn the wearer of danger or illness by changing color. It has been imitated by stained howlite, fossil bone or tooth, limestone, chalcedony, glass, and enamel. In 1972, an imitation turquoise was produced in France by Gilson.

GREEN FACE
This greenish blue turquoise stone has been carved in the image of a child's face, set in relief in a swivel ring.

PERSIAN BLUE
These two ornaments, engraved and inlaid with gold, are made from the finest sky blue turquoise, mined in Persia (now Iran) for over 3,000 years. The distinctive color is due to the presence of copper and traces of iron. Persian turquoise was introduced to Europe via Turkey – hence its name, derived from the word "Turkish."

pattern engraved and inlaid with gold

cut and polished as cabochon

laboratory-made stone has uniform color

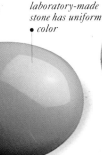

"spiderweb" turquoise has black veins

intense blue-green color

GILSON "SPIDERWEB" IMITATION

GILSON IMITATION

Bead   Cabochon   Cameo

thin crust of turquoise

TURQUOISE IN MATRIX

SG 2.80	RI 1.61–1.65	DR 0.040	Luster Waxy to dull

Crystal structure Triclinic	Composition Manganese silicate	Hardness 6

RHODONITE

Rhodonite has a distinct pink or rose red color, although material containing black veins is more popular than a uniform pink. Massive rhodonite is usually opaque to translucent and is carved or cut as cabochons or beads. Transparent crystals are rare and fragile, but some have been cut for collectors.

• **OCCURRENCE** Both crystals and massive material have been found in the Urals (Russia), Sweden, and Australia. Other localities for fine-grained rhodonite include Brazil, Mexico, the USA, Canada, Italy, India, Madagascar, South Africa, Japan, New Zealand, and England.

• **REMARK** The name comes from *rhodos*, the Greek for "rose," referring to the distinct color.

black-veined stones are the most • popular

characteristic pink-red color

massive habit •

OVAL CABOCHON

Bead   Cabochon   Cameo

black areas rich in manganese •

RHODONITE ROUGH

SG 3.60	RI 1.71–1.73	DR 0.014	Luster Vitreous

Crystal structure Triclinic	Composition Lithium aluminum hydroxyphosphate	Hardness 6

AMBLYGONITE

Amblygonite is found in a wide range of colors from white, pink, green, and blue to golden yellow and, more rarely, colorless. Large transparent to translucent crystals may occur, but as amblygonite is relatively soft, they are cut solely for collectors. Amblygonite is also found as cleavable or compact masses.

• **OCCURRENCE** Amblygonite is found in pegmatites. Brazil is the source of most gem-quality material, but it is also found in the USA. A pale mauve variety occurs in Namibia.

• **REMARK** Amblygonite has been confused with brazilianite and scapolite.

dark yellow • color

stones are too soft to be popular for jewelry

OVAL BRILLIANT CUT

straw yellow color is most common •

pale yellow • color

OVAL BRILLIANT CUT

perfect cleavage •

Brilliant   Brilliant   Mixed

INCOMPLETE CRYSTAL

SG 3.02	RI 1.57–1.60	DR 0.026	Luster Vitreous

Crystal structure Triclinic	Composition Complex borosilicate	Hardness 7

AXINITE

Axinite gets its name from its sharp-edged, axhead-shaped crystals. Although attractive and hard, they are brittle and rarely flaw-less and are faceted for collectors only. Brown is the most usual color, although it also occurs in honey yellow and plum purple varieties. A rare Tanzanian axinite is blue. Axinite is strongly pleochroic.

• **OCCURRENCE** Axinite is found in cavities in granite and in metamorphic rocks. Localities include New Jersey, where the attractive honey yellow crystals are found, Mexico, Cornwall (England), France, and in the gem gravels of Sri Lanka.

• **REMARK** Darker axinite has been confused with smoky quartz.

iron gives stone its rich • brown color

OVAL STEP CUT

fragile, sharp-edged crystals •

pale blue color due to low iron • content

BRILLIANT CUT

AXINITE CRYSTALS

Brilliant	Brilliant	Mixed

SG 3.28	RI 1.67–1.70	DR 0.011	Luster Vitreous

Crystal structure Triclinic	Composition Aluminum silicate	Hardness 5 or 7

KYANITE

Gem-quality kyanite crystals are pale to deep blue or white, gray, or green. Color dis-tribution in crystals may be uneven, with darker blue patches towards the interior.

• **OCCURRENCE** Kyanite is found in metamorphic gneiss and schist and in pegmatite veins through metamorphic rocks. It may be weathered out into alluvial deposits. Gem-quality crystals are found in Myanmar, Brazil, Kenya, and the European Alps. Alluvial deposits are found in India, Australia, and Kenya, and in parts of the USA.

• **REMARK** Kyanite crystals have two hardness values: they are softer parallel to the direction of cleavage and harder perpendicular to it.

cracks due to formation at high pressure •

rich blue • color

RECTANGULAR STEP CUT

uneven color • distribution

staurolite crystals commonly occur with kyanite •

kyanite crystals •

CRYSTAL

CRYSTALS IN MATRIX

Baguette	Step	Cabochon

SG 3.68	RI 1.71–1.73	DR 0.017	Luster Vitreous to pearly

Crystal structure Amorphous	Composition Hydrated silica gel	Hardness 6

OPAL

Opal is a hardened silica gel, usually containing 5–10 percent water. It is therefore noncrystalline, unlike most other gemstones, and may eventually dry out and crack. There are two varieties: precious opal, which shows flashes of color (iridescence), depending on the angle of viewing; and common or "potch" opal, which is often opaque and displays no iridescence. The iridescence of precious opal is caused by the way the structure, a regular arrangement of tiny silica spheres, diffracts light – the larger the spheres, the greater the range of colors. Precious opal occurs in a number of color varieties, some of which are shown here.

• **OCCURRENCE** Opal fills cavities in sedimentary rocks or veins in igneous rocks. It forms stalagmites or stalactites and replaces organic material in fossil wood, shell, and bone. Australia has been the main producer of opals since the 19th century. Other localities include Czechoslovakia, the USA, Brazil, Mexico, and southern Africa.

• **REMARK** Opals have been imitated by Slocum stone, a tough, manmade glass, and, in 1973, Gilson made an imitation opal in the laboratory (see p.36).

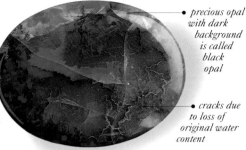

precious opal with dark background is called black opal

cracks due to loss of original water content

BLACK PRECIOUS OPAL

high-quality black opal from Australia

matrix •

BLACK PRECIOUS OPAL IN MATRIX

good-quality stones are transparent, not milky

beautiful, rich orange body color gives fire opal its name

FIRE OPAL BRILLIANT

transparent fire opal •

volcanic rhyolite matrix •

opaque white opal •

OPAL IN MATRIX

FIRE OPAL RING
Although many opals are cut *en cabochon*, this transparent fire opal has been faceted as an octagonal step cut and set in a gold ring.

SG 2.10	RI 1.37–1.47	DR None	Luster Vitreous

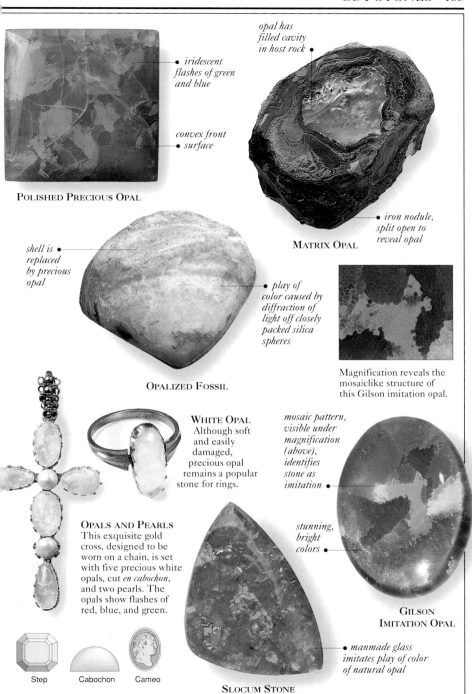

iridescent flashes of green and blue

convex front surface

POLISHED PRECIOUS OPAL

opal has filled cavity in host rock

MATRIX OPAL

iron nodule, split open to reveal opal

shell is replaced by precious opal

play of color caused by diffraction of light off closely packed silica spheres

OPALIZED FOSSIL

Magnification reveals the mosaiclike structure of this Gilson imitation opal.

WHITE OPAL
Although soft and easily damaged, precious opal remains a popular stone for rings.

mosaic pattern, visible under magnification (above), identifies stone as imitation

OPALS AND PEARLS
This exquisite gold cross, designed to be worn on a chain, is set with five precious white opals, cut *en cabochon*, and two pearls. The opals show flashes of red, blue, and green.

stunning, bright colors

Step   Cabochon   Cameo

GILSON IMITATION OPAL

manmade glass imitates play of color of natural opal

SLOCUM STONE

Crystal structure Amorphous	Composition Mainly silicon dioxide	Hardness 5

OBSIDIAN

Obsidian is a natural glass. It is formed from volcanic lava that cooled too quickly for significant crystallization to occur. Hence it is amorphous, with no cleavage; fracture is conchoidal. Obsidian is usually black, but brown, gray, and, more rarely, red, blue, and green material is found. The color may be uniform, striped, or spotted. Some inclusions give obsidian a metallic sheen, while internal bubbles or crystals (called crystallites) produce a "snowflake" effect (called snowflake obsidian) or an iridescence seen as flashes of color.

• **OCCURRENCE** Obsidian is found in areas where there is or has been volcanic activity, such as Hawaii, Japan, and Java. Other localities include Iceland, Hungary, the Lipari Islands off Italy, the former USSR, Mexico, Ecuador, and Guatemala. Dark nodules found in Arizona and New Mexico are called "Apache tears."

• **REMARK** Obsidian has been used since prehistoric times for making tools, weapons, masks, mirrors, and jewelry. The very sharp shards of the natural glass have been fashioned as blades, arrowheads, and daggers. Today most obsidian jewelry comes from North and Central America.

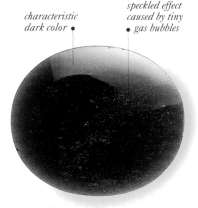

characteristic dark color

speckled effect caused by tiny gas bubbles

OBSIDIAN CABOCHON

rare red obsidian

banding caused by solidification of flowing lava

POLISHED OBSIDIAN SLICE

polished specimen has smooth, glassy surface

rough specimen has uneven surface

APACHE TEARS

mineral-lined cavities, called spherules

amorphous black obsidian

OBSIDIAN ROUGH

Cabochon

Polished

SG 2.35	RI 1.48–1.51	DR None	Luster Vitreous

Crystal structure Amorphous	Composition Mainly silicon dioxide	Hardness 5

TEKTITES

The first tektites were found in 1787 in the Moldau River in Czechoslovakia, hence their original name of "moldavites." Other color varieties of this natural glass have since been found in many different localities. Tektites are usually translucent and occur in a range of colors from green to brown. Their surfaces are usually uneven or rough, with a distinctive lumpy, jagged, or scarred texture. Tektites do not contain the crystallites found in obsidian (opposite). They may, however, have characteristic inclusions of round or torpedo-shaped bubbles or honeylike swirls.

• OCCURRENCE The Moldau River in Czechoslovakia is now the only known locality for green, transparent tektite. Tektites from Thailand have been carved as small, decorative objects worn in the belief that they give protection from evil.

• REMARK Several ideas have been put forward to explain the mysterious origin of tektites. One theory is that they came to Earth from outer space, melting as they passed through the atmosphere and thus forming their characteristic shape and surface texture. A second theory is that the impact of a large meteorite caused the surrounding rocks to melt and scatter, with cracks and scars then appearing as they cooled.

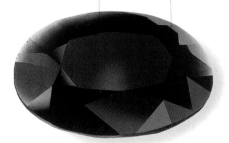

dark brown, semi-translucent stone

dark stones are faceted only rarely

OVAL BRILLIANT CUT

button shape caused by the way molten glass has cooled

TEKTITE ROUGH

surface shows cooling cracks

tektite varieties are named after their place of origin

AUSTRALITE ROUGH

stone may be confused with diopside because of green color

green, transparent material is most suitable for faceting

distinctive craggy, uneven surface

MOLDAVITE BRILLIANT CUT

translucent and transparent in parts

MOLDAVITE ROUGH

Brilliant

Cushion

Bead

SG 2.40	RI 1.48–1.51	DR None	Luster Vitreous

Crystal structure Orthorhombic	Composition Calcium carbonate, conchiolin, and water	Hardness 3

PEARL

Pearls are formed in shellfish – especially oysters and mussels – as a natural defense against an irritant such as a piece of grit. Layers of aragonite, known as nacre, are secreted around the irritant and gradually build up to form the solid pearl. Light reflecting from these overlapping layers produces a characteristic iridescent luster, also known as the "orient of pearl." An irritant is introduced to initiate the formation of a cultured pearl. In a "nucleated" cultured pearl a small bead is used as the nucleus upon which the layers of nacre are secreted. Pearls vary in color from white, or white with a hint of color (often pink), to brown or black, depending on the type of mollusk and the water. They are sensitive to acids, dryness, and humidity, and so are less durable than many other gems.

• OCCURRENCE Natural pearls have been harvested from the Persian Gulf, the Gulf of Manaar (Indian Ocean), and the Red Sea for thousands of years. The coasts of Polynesia and Australia produce mainly cultured pearls. Both freshwater and saltwater pearls are cultivated in Japan and China. Freshwater pearls occur in the rivers of Scotland, Ireland, France, Austria, Germany, and the USA (Mississippi).

• REMARK Pearls were once thought to be the tears of the gods.

pearl color is a mixture of body color and luster

pearl of Strombus gigas

NATURAL PINK PEARL

pearl of Tridacna gigas

NATURAL WHITE PEARL

brick colored where attached to shell

pearls form as spheres when irritant is not attached to shell

pinkish tinge

NATURAL FRESHWATER PEARLS

shell of the pearl oyster (Pinctada maxima)

irregular shapes may develop if irritant is attached to shell

natural white pearl

mother-of-pearl lining

iridescent, "pearly" luster

NATURAL FRESHWATER PEARLS

NATURAL PEARL IN OYSTER SHELL

SG 2.71	RI 1.53–1.68	DR Not applicable	Luster Pearly

A "BOMBAY BUNCH"
For hundreds of years, Bombay has been an important center for the buying and selling of pearls. To present them for selling, pearls are sorted by size, then strung into bunches on silk thread.

different sizes are included so that a complete necklace can be made from a "bunch" •

pearl buddhas formed on casts placed • *inside shell*

BUDDHA PEARLS
To produce miniature images of the Buddha, tiny casts were placed into the shell of this pearl mussel (*Cristaria plicata*). The mussel laid down nacreous layers over the casts, forming "blister" pearls. The pearls are later removed and the backs hidden in the mount or covered with mother-of-pearl.

JAPANESE CULTURE
This necklace, made by the Mikimoto company of Japan, uses saltwater cultured pearls. Japan leads the world in the production of cultured pearls, although they have been used by the Chinese for hundreds of years.

• *cultured pearls have the same pearly luster as natural specimens*

silver-wire • *tassels*

Bead

Crystal structure Amorphous	Composition Variety of lignite	Hardness 2½

JET

Jet is organic in origin. Like coal, it was formed from the remains of wood immersed in stagnant water millions of years ago, then compacted and fossilized by the pressures of burial. Jet is black or dark brown but may contain pyrite inclusions, which have a brassy color and metallic luster. Jet takes a good polish and is often faceted. When burned or touched with a hot needle, it exudes the characteristic smell of coal.

• **OCCURRENCE** Evidence suggests that jet has been mined since about 1400 BC, and worked pieces of jet have been found in prehistoric burial mounds. During the Roman occupation of the British Isles, worked pieces of jet were shipped to Rome. Perhaps the most famous historical source is Whitby in Yorkshire, England, where much of the jet that was so popular for the mourning jewelry of the 19th century originated. During this time the mining and fashioning of jet provided the town with much of its income. Other localities include Spain, France, Germany, Poland, India, Turkey, the former USSR, China, and the USA.

• **REMARK** Jet was popular for mourning jewelry in the 19th century because of its somber color and modest appearance, and it has been traditionally fashioned into rosaries for monks. Jet has also been known as black amber, as it may induce an electric charge like that of amber when rubbed. Powdered jet added to water or wine was believed to have medicinal powers.

Because jet is organic, it may dry out, causing the surface to crack.

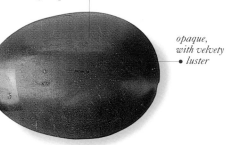

gems made from jet take a good polish •

opaque, with velvety • luster

OVAL CABOCHON

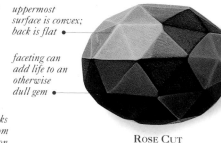

uppermost surface is convex; back is flat •

faceting can add life to an otherwise dull gem •

ROSE CUT

triangular facets •

surface cracks resulting from • dehydration

fine-grained, fragile specimen with rough, cracked surfaces •

dull, earthy luster before polishing •

DRILLED AND FACETED BEAD

SG 1.33	RI 1.64–1.68	DR Not applicable	Luster Velvety to waxy

VICTORIAN EARRINGS
Jet is light to wear, and so it is particularly suitable for earrings. It was very popular for mourning jewelry in Victorian England.

BLACK ROSE
This piece of carved Whitby jet, with a finely wrought rose at the center, dates from the latter part of the 19th century.

FOSSIL-BEARING JET
The ammonite and bivalve fossils trapped in this jet specimen are evidence of its organic origin.

JET PENDANT
This exquisite pendant of a dove with a heart in its beak shows how well jet can be carved and polished.

ammonite fossil •

• bivalve fossil

highly polished beads •

TURKISH BEADS
This necklace from eastern Turkey is made from beads of polished and drilled jet. The high polish has given the beads an attractive luster.

Bead

Cameo

Polished

Crystal structure Trigonal	Composition Calcium carbonate or conchiolin	Hardness 3

CORAL

Coral is made up of the skeletal remains of marine animals called coral polyps. These tiny creatures live in colonies that form branching structures as they grow, eventually forming coral reefs and atolls. The surface of these coral "branches" has a distinctive pattern made by the original animals – either striped or like wood grain. Most corals – red, pink, white, and blue varieties – are made of calcium carbonate; black and golden corals are made of a hornlike substance called conchiolin. Red coral is the most valuable and has been used in jewelry for thousands of years. Dull at first, all coral has a vitreous luster when polished but is sensitive to heat and acids and may fade with wear. Coral may be imitated by porcelain, stained bone, glass, plastic, or rubber and gypsum mixtures.

• **OCCURRENCE** Most precious coral is found in warm waters. Japanese coral is red, pink, or white. Red and pink coral is also found on the Mediterranean and African coasts, the Red Sea, and the waters off Malaysia and Japan. Black and golden coral is found off the coasts of the West Indies, Australia, and the Pacific islands.

• **REMARK** Coral has been said to protect children, and parents may still give a gift of coral to their young children.

vivid red
• color

• high polish
shows vitreous
luster

RED CORAL CABOCHON

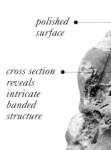

polished •
surface

cross section •
reveals
intricate
banded
structure

RED CORAL SLICE

• branches
form from
coral polyp
skeletons

red coral
from the
Mediterranean •

• distinctive "wood
grain" pattern on
surface of branches

RED CORAL

RED CORAL CARVING
This piece of red coral (*Corallium rubrum*) from the Mediterranean has been carved to show a monkey climbing a blossoming tree.

SG 2.68	RI 1.49–1.66	DR Not applicable	Luster Dull to vitreous

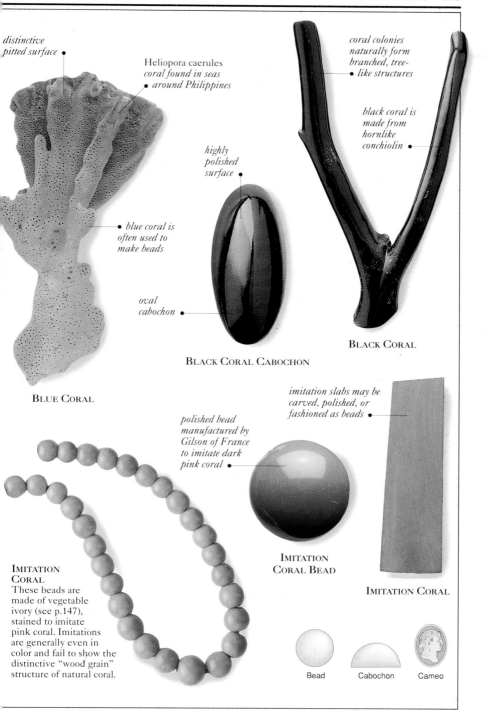

distinctive
pitted surface

Heliopora caerules
coral found in seas
around Philippines

highly
polished
surface

blue coral is
often used to
make beads

oval
cabochon

coral colonies
naturally form
branched, tree-
like structures

black coral is
made from
hornlike
conchiolin

BLACK CORAL CABOCHON

BLACK CORAL

BLUE CORAL

imitation slabs may be
carved, polished, or
fashioned as beads

polished bead
manufactured by
Gilson of France
to imitate dark
pink coral

**IMITATION
CORAL**
These beads are
made of vegetable
ivory (see p.147),
stained to imitate
pink coral. Imitations
are generally even in
color and fail to show the
distinctive "wood grain"
structure of natural coral.

**IMITATION
CORAL BEAD**

IMITATION CORAL

Bead   Cabochon   Cameo

Crystal structure Various	Composition Calcium carbonate	Hardness 2½

SHELL

Shells come in a wide variety of sizes, shapes, and colors and may be fashioned into beads, buttons, jewelry, inlay, knife handles, snuff boxes, and other decorative items. Conch shells with pink and white layers may be carved into intricate and attractive cameos, as may helmet shells, which have white outer layers and golden brown or orange inner layers. The large pearl oysters (*Pinctada maxima* and *P. margaritifera*), abalones (paua), and topshells (Trochidae) are all prized for their iridescent (mother-of-pearl) shell linings. Tortoiseshell comes not from the tortoise but from the hard shell (carapace) of the Hawksbill Turtle. It has rich brown mottling or flamelike patterns on a warm, translucent, golden yellow background and is fashioned by warming the shell to flatten it and to scrape off the ridges. It is then polished and cut to shape.
• **OCCURRENCE** *Pinctada* oysters are found off northern Australia. Abalones are found off the coasts of the USA and paua shells off New Zealand. The Hawksbill Turtle is found in the warm waters of Indonesia and the West Indies.
• **REMARK** Tortoiseshell has now been largely replaced by plastic imitations.

TIGER COWRIE CAMEO
This Asian woman has been carved in a Tiger Cowrie shell (*Cypraea tigris*). The different colored layers have been cut away to create the effect of foreground and background.

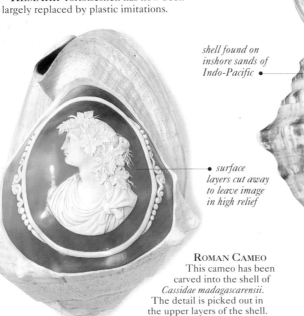

bright pink interior may be used for inlay work •

shell found on inshore sands of Indo-Pacific •

• *surface layers cut away to leave image in high relief*

ROMAN CAMEO
This cameo has been carved into the shell of *Cassidae madagascarensii*. The detail is picked out in the upper layers of the shell.

SPIDER CONCH
(*LAMBIS LAMBIS*)

SG 1.30	RI 1.53–1.69	DR Not applicable	Luster Dull to vitreous

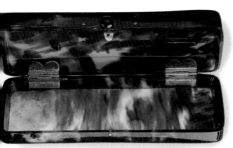

HINGED BOX
The lid and base of this box show the distinctive coloring and patterning of tortoiseshell. Some light areas are transparent to semi-translucent; darker areas are opaque.

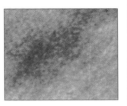

When magnified, spots can be seen in natural but not in imitation tortoiseshell.

distinctive rich brown mottling

HAIR COMB
This tortoise-shell comb shows attractive, almost fiery, patterns of yellow and brown, with darker patches.

ridges are scraped away during fashioning

iridescent colors are prized in many forms of jewelry and decorative items

nacreous lining is used for jewelry and inlays

TORTOISESHELL (CARAPACE OF HAWKSBILL TURTLE)

SHELL PILLBOX
The inlay in the lid of this pillbox has been fashioned from the layered, iridescent lining of a shell from the Haliotis family of shellfish.

MOTHER-OF-PEARL SHELL

Cabochon   Cameo   Polished

Crystal structure Amorphous	Composition Calcium hydroxyphosphate and organic	Hardness 2½

IVORY

Ivory has been prized for thousands of years for its rich, creamy color, its fine texture, and its ease of carving. Until quite recently it was a popular material for both jewelry and ornaments, but international restrictions on trading now help to protect the animals from which ivory is taken. The teeth or tusks of mammals all have ivory as a constituent. Although usually associated with elephants, ivory from the Hippopotamus, Wild Boar, and Warthog is also used. Marine mammals such as the Sperm Whale, Walrus, Sea Lion, and Narwhal have ivory as well. Fossil ivory – from prehistoric animals such as mammoths, mastodons, or dinosaurs – can also be carved.

• **OCCURRENCE** African Elephants' ivory is the most highly valued, with a warm tint and little grain or mottling. Indian Elephants' ivory is a denser white, softer, and easier to work, but it yellows more easily. Ivory markets include Europe, Myanmar, and Indonesia.

• **REMARK** One piece of carved mammoth ivory found in France is estimated to be over 30,000 years old. In China and Japan ivory carving remains popular, even today. However, elsewhere, the use of ivory simulants – bone, horn, jasper, vegetable ivory, plastic, and resin – has been strongly encouraged in order to protect ivory-bearing animals.

INDIAN ELEPHANT IVORY
This intricately fashioned scene was probably carved from the tusk of an Indian Elephant, whose ivory is softer and whiter than the African Elephant's.

distinctive curved growth lines •

thin canals containing nerve fibers •

AFRICAN ELEPHANT IVORY
Made from warm, mellow African Elephant ivory, this Roman head is worked in the style popular in the 4th to 5th century BC.

cut and polished molar tooth •

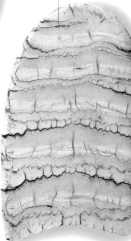

ELEPHANT IVORY CUP
Looking down into this cup, the crisscrossing, curving pattern unique to elephant ivory is visible.

POLISHED SECTION OF ELEPHANT TOOTH

SG 1.90	RI 1.53–1.54	DR Not applicable	Luster Dull to greasy

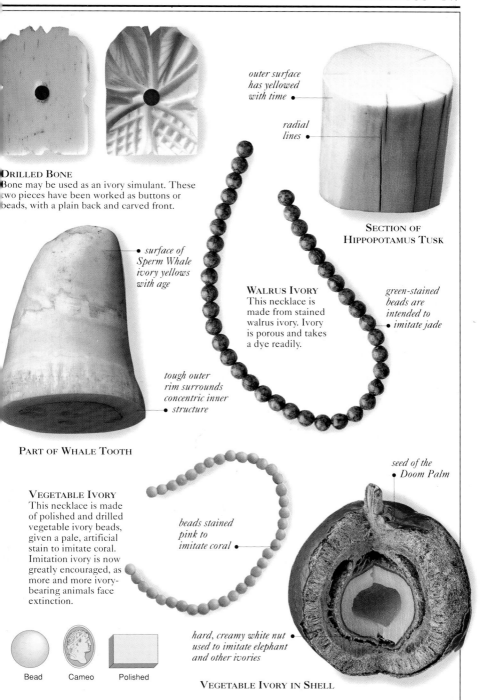

DRILLED BONE
Bone may be used as an ivory simulant. These two pieces have been worked as buttons or beads, with a plain back and carved front.

outer surface has yellowed with time •

radial lines •

SECTION OF HIPPOPOTAMUS TUSK

• surface of Sperm Whale ivory yellows with age

WALRUS IVORY
This necklace is made from stained walrus ivory. Ivory is porous and takes a dye readily.

green-stained beads are intended to • imitate jade

tough outer rim surrounds concentric inner • structure

PART OF WHALE TOOTH

seed of the • Doom Palm

VEGETABLE IVORY
This necklace is made of polished and drilled vegetable ivory beads, given a pale, artificial stain to imitate coral. Imitation ivory is now greatly encouraged, as more and more ivory-bearing animals face extinction.

beads stained pink to imitate coral •

Bead   Cameo   Polished

hard, creamy white nut • used to imitate elephant and other ivories

VEGETABLE IVORY IN SHELL

| Crystal structure Amorphous | Composition Mixture of organic plant resins | Hardness 2½ |

AMBER

Amber is the fossilized resin of trees. Most amber is golden yellow to golden orange, but green, red, violet, and black amber has been found. Transparent to translucent, it usually occurs as nodules or small, irregularly shaped masses, often with a cracked and weathered surface. Amber may contain insects (and more rarely frogs, toads, and lizards), moss, lichen, or pine needles that were trapped millions of years ago while the resin was still sticky. Air bubbles may give amber a cloudy appearance, but heating in oil will clear this. When rubbed, amber produces a negative electrical charge that attracts dust. "Ambroid" is formed by heating and pressing together scraps of amber.
• OCCURRENCE The most famous deposits are in the Baltic region, particularly along the coasts of Poland and the former USSR. Baltic amber (known as succinite) washed from the seabed may reach as far as the coasts of England, Norway, and Denmark. Amber from Myanmar is called burmite; Sicilian amber is known as simetite. Other localities include the Dominican Republic, Mexico, France, Spain, Italy, Germany, Romania, Canada, Czechoslovakia, and the USA.
• REMARK Amber has had a number of medicinal uses attributed to it, but today it is used almost exclusively for jewelry. It has been imitated by plastic, glass, synthetic resin, and other natural resins, like copal.

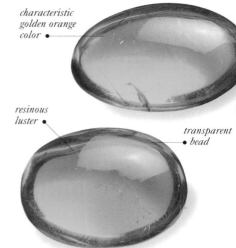

characteristic golden orange color •

resinous luster •

transparent • bead

POLISHED BEADS

cracks produce spangling effect •

cracks may be caused by heat • treatment

POLISHED "SUN-SPANGLED" BEAD

weathered surface •

• cloudy, opaque area

• transparent area

PARTLY POLISHED AMBER

pebble found washed up on beach •

BALTIC AMBER ROUGH

| SG 1.08 | RI 1.54–1.55 | DR Not applicable | Luster Resinous |

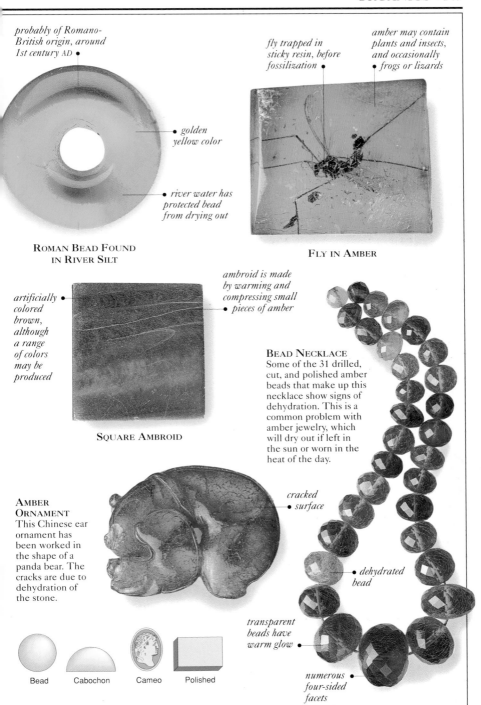

probably of Romano-British origin, around 1st century AD

golden yellow color

river water has protected bead from drying out

ROMAN BEAD FOUND IN RIVER SILT

fly trapped in sticky resin, before fossilization

amber may contain plants and insects, and occasionally frogs or lizards

FLY IN AMBER

artificially colored brown, although a range of colors may be produced

ambroid is made by warming and compressing small pieces of amber

SQUARE AMBROID

BEAD NECKLACE
Some of the 31 drilled, cut, and polished amber beads that make up this necklace show signs of dehydration. This is a common problem with amber jewelry, which will dry out if left in the sun or worn in the heat of the day.

cracked surface

AMBER ORNAMENT
This Chinese ear ornament has been worked in the shape of a panda bear. The cracks are due to dehydration of the stone.

dehydrated bead

transparent beads have warm glow

Bead   Cabochon   Cameo   Polished

numerous four-sided facets

TABLE OF PROPERTIES

THIS TABLE INCLUDES all of the technical information for each gem species, arranged alphabetically by gem name. By so doing, it is intended to give the reader an at-a-glance reference to the more important physical and optical properties of each gem species.

The chemical composition of each gem is shown here by a formula, which includes all essential elements of that gem. Composition may vary slightly, depending on locality and conditions of formation. The physical properties of the gems – their hardness and specific gravity – are given as mean (average) values. Hardness is denoted by a figure from the Mohs scale of hardness, a scale used to classify the hardness of minerals relative to one another. The intervals between successive values are unequal, and an intermediate value such as $3\frac{1}{2}$ denotes that the hardness is between 3 and 4, but it is not necessarily exactly halfway between. Hardness may vary slightly depending upon exact chemical content, so a mean figure is given here. The values for specific gravity (SG), which give an indication of the density of a gem, are also given as mean figures.

The optical properties of the gems are represented here by the refractive indices (RI) and the birefraction (DR).

They are related to crystal structure: a gem with cubic structure has a single value as its refractive index (RI); doubly refracting gems have two refractive indices (see p.21). Doubly refracting gems also have a value of birefraction (DR), found by using a refractometer. This figure is the difference between the highest and the lowest refractive indices. Physical and optical properties are continually reviewed as new minerals are discovered and new deposits exploited, so all figures given here are mean values, to be used as a guide only.

KEY TO CHEMICAL ELEMENTS IN THIS BOOK			
Al	ALUMINUM	Mg	MAGNESIUM
Ag	SILVER	Mn	MANGANESE
Au	GOLD	Na	SODIUM
B	BORON	O	OXYGEN
Ba	BARIUM	P	PHOSPHORUS
Be	BERYLLIUM	Pb	LEAD
C	CARBON	Pt	PLATINUM
Ca	CALCIUM	S	SULFUR
Cl	CHLORINE	Si	SILICON
Cr	CHROMIUM	Sn	TIN
Cu	COPPER	Sr	STRONTIUM
F	FLUORINE	Ti	TITANIUM
Fe	IRON	W	TUNGSTEN
H	HYDROGEN	Zn	ZINC
K	POTASSIUM	Zr	ZIRCONIUM
Li	LITHIUM		

NAME & CHEMICAL COMPOSITION	STRUCTURE	HARDNESS	SG	RI	DR
ACHROITE (TOURMALINE) $Na(Li,Al)_3Al_6(BO_3)_3Si_6O_{18}(OH)_4$	Trigonal	$7\frac{1}{2}$	3.06	1.62–1.64	0.018
AGATE (CHALCEDONY) SiO_2	Trigonal	7	2.61	1.53–1.54	0.004
ALBITE $(Na,Ca)AlSi_3O_8$	Triclinic	6	2.64	1.54–1.55	0.009
ALMANDINE (GARNET) $Fe_3Al_2(SiO_4)_3$	Cubic	$7\frac{1}{2}$	4.00	1.76–1.83	None
AMBER mainly $C_{10}H_{16}O$	Amorphous	$2\frac{1}{2}$	1.08	1.54–1.55	N/A

Name & Chemical Composition	Structure	Hardness	SG	RI	DR
AMBLYGONITE $LiAl(F,OH)PO_4$	Triclinic	6	3.02	1.57–1.60	0.026
AMETHYST (QUARTZ) SiO_2	Trigonal	7	2.65	1.54–1.55	0.009
ANDALUSITE Al_2SiO_5	Orthorhombic	7½	3.16	1.63–1.64	0.010
ANDRADITE GARNET $Ca_3Fe_2(SiO_4)_3$	Cubic	6½	3.85	1.85–1.89	None
ANGLESITE $PbSO_4$	Orthorhombic	3	6.35	1.87–1.89	0.017
APATITE $Ca(F,Cl)Ca_4(PO_4)_3$	Hexagonal	5	3.20	1.63–1.64	0.003
AQUAMARINE (BERYL) $Be_3Al_2(SiO_3)_6$	Hexagonal	7½	2.69	1.57–1.58	0.006
ARAGONITE $CaCO_3$	Orthorhombic	3½	2.94	1.53–1.68	0.155
AVENTURINE QUARTZ SiO_2	Trigonal	7	2.65	1.54–1.55	0.009
AXINITE $CaFeMgBAl_2Si_4O_{15}(OH)$	Triclinic	7	3.28	1.67–1.70	0.011
AZURITE $Cu_3(OH)_2(CO_3)_2$	Monoclinic	3½	3.77	1.73–1.84	0.110
BARITE $BaSO_4$	Orthorhombic	3	4.45	1.63–1.65	0.012
BENITOITE $BaTiSi_3O_9$	Hexagonal	6½	3.67	1.76–1.80	0.047
BERYLLONITE $NaBePO_4$	Monoclinic	5½	2.83	1.55–1.56	0.009
BLOODSTONE (CHALCEDONY) SiO_2	Trigonal	7	2.61	1.53–1.54	0.004
BRAZILIANITE $Al_3Na(PO_4)_2(OH)_4$	Monoclinic	5½	2.99	1.60–1.62	0.021
BROWN QUARTZ (SMOKY QUARTZ) SiO_2	Trigonal	7	2.65	1.54–1.55	0.009
CALCITE $CaCO_3$	Trigonal	3	2.71	1.48–1.66	0.172
CARNELIAN (CHALCEDONY) SiO_2	Trigonal	7	2.61	1.53–1.54	0.004
CASSITERITE SnO_2	Tetragonal	6½	6.95	2.00–2.10	0.100
CELESTINE $SrSO_4$	Orthorhombic	3½	3.98	1.62–1.63	0.010
CERUSSITE $PbCO_3$	Orthorhombic	3½	6.51	1.80–2.08	0.274
CHALCEDONY SiO_2	Trigonal	7	2.61	1.53–1.54	0.004
CHATOYANT QUARTZ SiO_2	Trigonal	7	2.65	1.54–1.55	0.009
CHRYSOBERYL $BeAl_2O_4$	Orthorhombic	8½	3.71	1.74–1.75	0.009

Name & Chemical Composition	Structure	Hardness	SG	RI	DR
CHRYSOCOLLA $(Cu,Al)_2H_2Si_2O_5(OH)_4.nH_2O$	Monoclinic	2	2.20	1.57–1.63	0.030
CHRYSOPRASE (CHALCEDONY) SiO_2	Trigonal	7	2.61	1.53–1.54	0.004
CITRINE (QUARTZ) SiO_2	Trigonal	7	2.65	1.54–1.55	0.009
CORAL $CaCO_3$ (or $C_3H_{48}N_9O_{11}$)	Trigonal	3	2.68	1.49–1.66	N/A
DANBURITE $CaB_2(SiO_4)_2$	Orthorhombic	7	3.00	1.63–1.64	0.006
DATOLITE $Ca(B,OH)SiO_4$	Monoclinic	5	2.95	1.62–1.65	0.044
DIAMOND C	Cubic	10	3.52	2.42	None
DIOPSIDE $CaMg(SiO_3)_2$	Monoclinic	5½	3.29	1.66–1.72	0.029
DIOPTASE $CuOSiO_2H_2O$	Trigonal	5	3.31	1.67–1.72	0.053
DOLOMITE $CaMg(CO_3)_2$	Trigonal	3½	2.85	1.50–1.68	0.179
DRAVITE (TOURMALINE) $NaMg_3Al_6(BO_3)_3Si_6O_{18}(OH)_4$	Trigonal	7½	3.06	1.61–1.63	0.018
DUMORTIERITE $Al_7(BO_3)(SiO_4)_3O_3$	Orthorhombic	7	3.28	1.69–1.72	0.037
EMERALD (BERYL) $Be_3Al_2(SiO_3)_6$	Hexagonal	7½	2.71	1.57–1.58	0.006
ENSTATITE $Mg_2Si_2O_6$	Orthorhombic	5½	3.27	1.66–1.67	0.010
EPIDOTE $Ca_2(Al,Fe)_3(OH)(SiO_4)_3$	Monoclinic	6½	3.40	1.74–1.78	0.035
EUCLASE $Be(Al,OH)SiO_4$	Monoclinic	7½	3.10	1.65–1.67	0.019
FIRE AGATE (CHALCEDONY) SiO_2	Trigonal	7	2.61	1.53–1.54	0.004
FLUORITE CaF_2	Cubic	4	3.18	1.43	None
GOLD Au	Cubic	2½	19.30	None	None
GOSHENITE (BERYL) $Be_3Al_2(SiO_3)_6$	Hexagonal	7½	2.80	1.58–1.59	0.008
GROSSULAR (GARNET) $Ca_3Al_2(SiO_4)_3$	Cubic	7	3.49	1.69–1.73	None
GYPSUM $CaSO_4.2H_2O$	Monoclinic	2	2.32	1.52–1.53	0.010
HAMBERGITE $Be_2(OH)BO_3$	Orthorhombic	7½	2.35	1.55–1.63	0.072
HAUYNE $(Na,Ca)_{4–8}Al_6Si_6(O,S)_{24}(SO_4Cl)_{1–2}$	Cubic	6	2.40	1.50 (mean)	None
HELIODOR (BERYL) $Be_3Al_2(SiO_3)_6$	Hexagonal	7½	2.80	1.57–1.58	0.005

Name & Chemical Composition	Structure	Hardness	SG	RI	DR
HEMATITE Fe_2O_3	Trigonal	6½	5.20	2.94–3.22	0.280
HESSONITE (GROSSULAR GARNET) $Ca_3Al_2(SiO_4)_3$	Cubic	7¼	3.65	1.73–1.75	None
HOWLITE $C_2B_5SiO_9(OH)_5$	Monoclinic	3½	2.58	1.58–1.59	0.022
HYPERSTHENE $(Fe,Mg)SiO_3$	Orthorhombic	5½	3.35	1.65–1.67	0.010
INDICOLITE (TOURMALINE) $Na(Li,Al)_3Al_6(BO_3)_3Si_6O_{18}(OH)_4$	Trigonal	7½	3.06	1.62–1.64	0.018
IOLITE $Mg_2Al_4Si_5O_{18}$	Orthorhombic	7	2.63	1.53–1.55	0.010
IVORY $Ca_5(PO_4)_3(OH)$ and organic material	Amorphous	2½	1.90	1.53–1.54	N/A
JADEITE (JADE) $Na(Al,Fe)Si_2O_6$	Monoclinic	7	3.33	1.66–1.68	0.012
JASPER (CHALCEDONY) SiO_2	Trigonal	7	2.61	1.53–1.54	0.004
JET Lignite	Amorphous	2½	1.33	1.64–1.68	N/A
KORNERUPINE $Mg_4(Al,Fe)_6(Si,B)_4O_{21}(OH)$	Orthorhombic	6½	3.32	1.66–1.68	0.013
KYANITE Al_2SiO_5	Triclinic	5 or 7	3.68	1.71–1.73	0.017
LABRADORITE $(Na,Ca)(Al,Si)_4O_8$	Triclinic	6	2.70	1.56–1.57	0.010
LAPIS LAZULI (LAZURITE) $(Na,Ca)_8(Al,Si)_{12}O_{24}(SO_4)Cl_2(OH)_2$	Various	5½	2.80	1.50 (mean)	None
LAZULITE $MgAl_2(PO_4)_2(OH)_2$	Monoclinic	5½	3.10	1.61–1.64	0.031
MALACHITE $Cu_2(OH)_2CO_3$	Monoclinic	4	3.80	1.85 (mean)	0.025
MEERSCHAUM $Mg_4Si_6O_{15}(OH)_2.6H_2O$	Monoclinic	2½	1.50	1.51–1.53	None
MICROCLINE $KAlSi_3O_8$	Triclinic	6	2.56	1.52–1.53	0.008
MILKY QUARTZ SiO_2	Trigonal	7	2.65	1.54–1.55	0.009
MOONSTONE (ORTHOCLASE) $KAlSi_3O_8$	Monoclinic	6	2.57	1.52–1.53	0.005
MORGANITE (BERYL) $Be_3Al_2(SiO_3)_6$	Hexagonal	7½	2.80	1.58–1.59	0.008
NEPHRITE (JADE) $Ca_2(Mg,Fe)_5Si_3O_{22}(OH)_2$	Monoclinic	6½	2.96	1.61–1.63	0.027
OBSIDIAN Mainly SiO_2	Amorphous	5	2.35	1.48–1.51	None
OLIGOCLASE $(Na,Ca)(Al,Si)_4O_8$	Triclinic	6	2.64	1.54–1.55	0.007
ONYX SiO_2	Trigonal	7	2.61	1.53–1.54	0.004

Name & Chemical Composition	Structure	Hardness	SG	RI	DR
OPAL $SiO_2.nH_2O$	Amorphous	6	2.10	1.37–1.47	None
ORTHOCLASE $KAlSi_3O_8$	Monoclinic	6	2.56	1.51–1.54	0.005
PADPARADSCHA (CORUNDUM) Al_2O_3	Trigonal	9	4.00	1.76–1.77	0.008
PEARL $CaCO_3,C_3H_{18}N_9O_{11}.nH_2O$	Orthorhombic	3	2.71	1.53–1.68	N/A
PERIDOT $(Mg,Fe)_2SiO_4$	Orthorhombic	6½	3.34	1.64–1.69	0.036
PETALITE $Li_2OAl_2O_38SiO_2$	Monoclinic	6	2.42	1.50–1.51	0.014
PHENAKITE Be_2SiO_4	Trigonal	7½	2.96	1.65–1.67	0.015
PHOSPHOPHYLLITE $Zn_2(Fe,Mn)(PO_4)_2.4H_2O$	Monoclinic	3½	3.10	1.59–1.62	0.021
PLASMA (CHALCEDONY) SiO_2	Trigonal	7	2.61	1.53–1.54	0.004
PLATINUM Pt	Cubic	4	21.40	None	None
PRASE (CHALCEDONY) SiO_2	Trigonal	7	2.61	1.53–1.54	0.004
PREHNITE $Ca_2Al_2Si_3O_{10}(OH)_2$	Orthorhombic	6	2.87	1.61–1.64	0.016
PYRITE FeS_2	Cubic	6	4.90	None	None
PYROPE (GARNET) $Mg_3Al_2(SiO_4)_3$	Cubic	7¼	3.80	1.72–1.76	None
RHODOCHROSITE $MnCO_3$	Trigonal	4	3.60	1.60–1.80	0.220
RHODONITE $(Mn,Fe,Mg,Ca)SiO_3$	Triclinic	6	3.60	1.71–1.73	0.014
ROCK CRYSTAL (QUARTZ) SiO_2	Trigonal	7	2.65	1.54–1.55	0.009
ROSE QUARTZ SiO_2	Trigonal	7	2.65	1.54–1.55	0.009
RUBELLITE (TOURMALINE) $Na(Li,Al)_3Al_6(BO_3)_3Si_6O_{18}(OH)_4$	Trigonal	7½	3.06	1.62–1.64	0.018
RUBY (CORUNDUM) Al_2O_3	Trigonal	9	4.00	1.76–1.77	0.008
RUTILE TiO_2	Tetragonal	6	4.25	2.62–2.90	0.287
SAPPHIRE (CORUNDUM) Al_2O_3	Trigonal	9	4.00	1.76–1.77	0.008
SARD SiO_2	Trigonal	7	2.61	1.53–1.54	0.004
SARDONYX (CHALCEDONY) SiO_2	Trigonal	7	2.61	1.53–1.54	0.004
SCAPOLITE $Na_4Al_3Si_9O_{24}Cl–Ca_4Al_6Si_6O_{24}(CO_3,SO_4)$	Tetragonal	6	2.70	1.54–1.58	0.020

Name & Chemical Composition	Structure	Hardness	SG	RI	DR
SCHEELITE $CaWO_4$	Tetragonal	5	6.10	1.92–1.93	0.017
SCHORL (TOURMALINE) $NaFe_3Al_6(BO_3)_3Si_6O_{18}(OH)_4$	Trigonal	7½	3.06	1.62–1.67	0.018
SERPENTINE $Mg_6(OH)_8Si_4O_{10}$	Monoclinic	5	2.60	1.55–1.56	0.001
SHELL $CaCO_3$ and $C_{32}H_{48}N_2O_{11}$	Various	2½	1.30	1.53–1.59	N/A
SILLIMANITE Al_2SiO_5	Orthorhombic	7½	3.25	1.66–1.68	0.019
SILVER Ag	Cubic	2½	10.50	None	None
SINHALITE $Mg(Al,Fe)BO_4$	Orthorhombic	6½	3.48	1.67–1.71	0.038
SMITHSONITE $ZnCO_3$	Trigonal	5	4.35	1.62–1.85	0.230
SODALITE $3NaAlSiO_4NaCl$	Cubic	5½	2.27	1.48 (mean)	None
SPESSARTINE (GARNET) $Mn_3Al_2(SiO_4)_3$	Cubic	7	4.16	1.79–1.81	None
SPHALERITE $(Zn,Fe)S$	Cubic	3½	4.09	2.36–2.37	None
SPINEL $MgAl_2O_4$	Cubic	8	3.60	1.71–1.73	None
SPODUMENE $LiAl(SiO_3)_2$	Monoclinic	7	3.18	1.66–1.67	0.015
STAUROLITE $(Fe,Mg,Zn)_2Al_9(Si,Al)_4O_{22}(OH)_2$	Orthorhombic	7	3.72	1.74–1.75	0.013
TAAFFEITE $BeMg_3Al_8O_{16}$	Hexagonal	8	3.61	1.72–1.77	0.004
TEKTITES Mainly SiO_2	Amorphous	5	2.40	1.48–1.51	None
TITANITE (SPHENE) $CaTiSiO_5$	Monoclinic	5	3.53	1.84–2.03	0.120
TOPAZ $Al_2(F,OH)_2SiO_4$	Orthorhombic	8	3.54	1.62–1.63	0.010
TUGTUPITE $Na_4AlBeSi_4O_{12}Cl$	Tetragonal	6	2.40	1.49–1.50	0.006
TURQUOISE $CuAl_6(PO_4)_4(OH)_8.5H_2O$	Triclinic	6	2.80	1.61–1.65	0.040
UVAROVITE (GARNET) $Ca_3Cr_2(SiO_4)_3$	Cubic	7½	3.77	1.86–1.87	None
VESUVIANITE (IDOCRASE) $Ca_6Al(Al,OH)(SiO_4)_5$	Tetragonal	6½	3.40	1.70–1.75	0.005
WATERMELON TOURMALINE $Na(Li,Al)_3Al_6(BO_3)_3Si_6O_{18}(OH)_4$	Trigonal	7½	3.06	1.62–1.64	0.018
ZIRCON $ZrSiO_4$	Tetragonal	7½	4.69	1.93–1.98	0.059
ZOISITE $Ca_2(Al,OH)Al_2(SiO_4)_3$	Orthorhombic	6½	3.35	1.69–1.70	0.010

GLOSSARY

WORDS PRINTED in bold type have their own definition elsewhere in the glossary.

• **ABSORPTION SPECTRUM**
Pattern of dark lines or bands seen when a gem is viewed through a **spectroscope**.

• **ALLOCHROMATIC**
Refers to gems colored by impurities, without which the gem would be colorless.

• **ALLUVIAL DEPOSITS**
Concentrations of material that have been separated by weathering from the host **rock**, then deposited by rivers or streams.

• **AMORPHOUS**
Without a regular internal atomic structure or external shape.

• **ASSOCIATED MINERALS**
Minerals found growing together, though not necessarily **intergrown**.

• **ASTERISM**
Star effect seen on some stones when cut *en cabochon*.

• **BASAL PINACOID**
Feature relating to **crystal** symmetry. A **columnar** or **prismatic** crystal with flat ends may be referred to as having a basal pinacoid.

• **BIREFRACTION (DR)**
The difference between the highest and the lowest **refractive indices** in **doubly refractive** gems.

• **BOTRYOIDAL**
Shape similar to a bunch of grapes.

• **CABOCHON**
Gem cut and polished to have a domed upper surface. Such stones are said to be cut *en cabochon*.

• **CAMEO**
Design in low relief, around which the background has been cut away.

• **CARAT (CT)**
Unit of weight used for gems – a carat is one-fifth of a gram. It is also used to describe the purity of gold – pure gold is 24 carat.

• **CHATOYANCY**
The cat's-eye effect shown by some stones when cut *en cabochon*.

• **CLEAVAGE**
Breaking of a stone along lines of weakness related to the internal atomic structure. *See also* **Fracture**.

• **COLUMNAR**
Type of **habit** in which **crystals** form in the shape of columns (elongated prisms).

• **COMPOSITE STONE**
Stone assembled from several pieces, often to imitate a gem.

• **CONCHOIDAL FRACTURE**
Shell-like fracture. *See* **Fracture**.

• **CROWN**
Top part of a cut stone, above the **girdle**.

• **CRYPTOCRYSTALLINE**
Mineral structure in which **crystals** are so small they are not distinguishable with a microscope.

• **CRYSTAL**
Solid that has a definite internal atomic structure, producing a characteristic external shape and physical and optical properties.

• **CRYSTAL STRUCTURE**
Internal atomic structure of a **crystal**. All crystalline gems may be classified in one of seven groups, according to the symmetry of their structure: cubic, tetragonal, hexagonal, trigonal, orthorhombic, monoclinic, and triclinic.

• **CUT**
Term used to describe the way in which a **stone** is faceted. *See also* **Faceting**.

• **DICHROIC**
Refers to a gem that appears two different colors or shades when viewed from different directions.

• **DIFFRACTION**
The splitting of white light into its constituent spectral colors – the colors of the rainbow – when it passes through a hole or grating.

• **DISPERSION**
The splitting of white light into its constituent spectral colors – the rainbow colors – when it passes through inclined surfaces, such as those on a **prism** or **faceted** gem. Dispersion in gems is called fire.

• **DOUBLE REFRACTION (DR)**
Phenomenon in which each ray of light is split in two as it enters a noncubic **mineral**. Each ray travels at a different speed and has its own **refractive index**. *See also* **Birefraction**.

• **DOUBLET**
Composite stone made of two pieces cemented or glued together.

• **EVAPORITE DEPOSIT**
Sedimentary rock or **mineral** resulting from the evaporation of water from mineral-bearing fluids, usually seawater.

• **FACES**
Flat surfaces that make up the external shape of a **crystal**.

• **FACET**
Surface of a cut and polished gem.

• **FACETING**
Cutting and polishing of the surfaces of a **gemstone** into **facets**. The number and shape of the facets give the stone its style of **cut**.

• **FANCY CUT**
Name applied to a stone given an unconventional shape when cut.

• **FIRE**
See **Dispersion**.

• **FRACTURE**
Chipping or breaking of a stone in a way unconnected to the internal atomic structure. Because of this, fracture surfaces are usually uneven. *See also* **Cleavage**.

• **GEMSTONE**
Decorative material, usually a **mineral**, prized for some or all of the qualities of beauty, durability, and rarity. It is used synonymously with "gem" and "stone" throughout this book.

• **GEODE**
Cavity within a **rock**, in which **crystals** line the inner surface and grow toward the center.

• **GIRDLE**
Band around the widest part of a cut stone, where the **crown** meets the **pavilion**.

• **GRANITE**
Coarse-grained **igneous rock** comprising mainly quartz, feldspar, and mica.

• **HABIT**
Shape in which a **crystal** naturally occurs.

• **HARDNESS**
See **Mohs Scale of Hardness**.

• **HEAT TREATMENT**
Application of heat to a gem with the purpose of enhancing the color or clarity.

• **HYDROTHERMAL**
Refers to processes that involve the alteration or deposition of minerals by water heated by igneous activity.

• **IDIOCHROMATIC**
Describes gems whose color is due to elements that are an essential part of their chemical composition.

• **IGNEOUS ROCKS**
Rocks formed from erupted volcanic **lava** or solidified **magma**.

- **IMITATION GEMSTONE**
Material that has the outward
appearance of the gem it is
intended to imitate, but which has
different physical properties. *See
also* **Synthetic gemstone.**
- **INCLUSIONS**
Markings or foreign bodies found
within a stone. Some can be used
to identify a particular **species.**
- **INTAGLIO**
Design in which the subject is cut
lower than the background.
- **INTERGROWN**
When two or more **minerals** grow
together and become interlocked.
- **INTRUSIVE**
Igneous rock that has solidified
within other rocks, below the
Earth's surface.
- **IRIDESCENCE**
Reflection of light off internal
features in a gem, giving rise to a
rainbowlike play of colors.
- **LAPIDARY**
Craftsman who cuts and polishes
gemstones.
- **LAVA**
Molten **rock** erupted from
volcanoes. *See also* **Magma.**
- **LUSTER**
Shine or "look" of a gemstone due
to reflection of light off the surface.
- **MAGMA**
Rock in a molten state below the
Earth's surface. *See also* **Lava.**
- **MAMMILLATED**
Smooth, rounded shape.
- **MASSIVE**
Used to describe **minerals** that
have an indefinite shape, or that
consist of small **crystals** in masses.
- **MATRIX**
The **rock** in which a gem is found.
Also known as host or parent rock.
- **METAMICT**
Refers to material that is breaking
down from a crystalline to an
amorphous state, due to the
presence of radioactive elements.
- **METAMORPHIC ROCKS**
Rocks that have been changed by
heat and/or pressure to form new
rocks consisting of new **minerals.**
- **MICROCRYSTALLINE**
Mineral structure in which
crystals are too small to be
detected by the naked eye.
- **MINERALS**
Inorganic, naturally occurring
materials with a constant chemical
composition and regular internal
atomic structure.

- **MIXED CUT**
Cut in which the **facets** above and
below the **girdle** are styled in
different ways – usually **brilliant
cut** above and **step cut** below.
- **MOHS SCALE OF HARDNESS**
Measure of a **mineral's** hardness in
relation to other minerals, based on
its ability to resist scratching.
- **MULTICOLORED**
Used to describe single **crystals**
made of different colored parts.
- **OPALESCENCE**
Milky blue form of **iridescence.**
- **ORE**
Rock that contains metals capable
of being extracted commercially.
- **ORGANIC GEM**
Gem made by or derived from
living organisms.
- **PASTE**
Glass made to **imitate** gems.
- **PAVILION**
Lower part of a cut stone, below
the **girdle.**
- **PEGMATITE**
An **igneous rock** formed as
residual liquids from **magma** cool,
often forming large **crystals.**
- **PLACER DEPOSIT**
Concentrated (**secondary**) deposit
of minerals, usually in rivers or seas.
- **PLATY**
Habit characterized by flat, thin,
platelike **crystals.**
- **PLEOCHROIC**
Term used to describe a gem that
appears two or more different colors
or shades when viewed from
different directions.
- **POLYCRYSTALLINE**
Refers to a **mineral** made of many
small **crystals.**
- **PRIMARY DEPOSIT**
Material still in its original **rock.**
See also **Secondary deposit.**
- **PRISMATIC**
Habit in which parallel pairs of
rectangular **faces** form prisms.
- **PSEUDOMORPH**
One **mineral** occurring in the
crystal shape of another.
- **REFRACTION**
Bending of light as it passes from
air into a different medium.
- **REFRACTIVE INDEX (RI)**
Measure of the slowing down and
bending of light rays as they enter a
gemstone. May be used to identify
individual gem **species.**
- **REFRACTOMETER**
Apparatus used to measure the
refractive indices of gems.

- **RHOMB**
Shape much like a skewed cube.
- **ROCK**
Material made up of one or more
minerals.
- **ROUGH**
Term used to describe a **rock** or
crystal still in its natural state,
before **faceting** or polishing.
- **SCHILLER/SHEEN**
Form of **iridescence.**
- **SCHIST**
Metamorphic rock in which
the **crystals** are in parallel
arrangement.
- **SECONDARY DEPOSIT**
Gems or **minerals** that have been
separated from their original **rock**
and redeposited elsewhere. *See also*
Primary deposit.
- **SEDIMENTARY ROCKS**
Rocks formed by the consolidation
and hardening of **rock** fragments,
organic remains, or other material.
- **SPECIES**
Used in this book to refer to
individual gems that have distinct
characteristics which may be
defined and verified.
- **SPECIFIC GRAVITY (SG)**
Density, measured as the weight of
the material compared with that of
an equal volume of water.
- **SPECTROSCOPE**
Instrument used to view the
absorption spectra of **gemstones.**
- **STEP CUT (OR TRAP CUT)**
Cut characterized by a rectangular
table facet and **girdle,** with rect-
angular facets parallel to these.
- **STONE**
Term used for any **gemstone.**
- **STRIATION**
Parallel scratch, groove, or line.
- **SYMMETRY, AXIS OF**
Imaginary line through a **crystal.** If
the crystal were rotated about its
axis it would present an identical
aspect two or more times in a
rotation of 360 degrees.
- **SYNTHETIC GEMSTONE**
Laboratory-made stone whose
chemical composition and optical
properties are similar to those of its
natural equivalent.
- **TABLE FACET**
Central **facet** on a gem's **crown.**
- **TRICHROIC**
Refers to a gem that appears three
different colors or shades when
viewed from different directions.
- **VITREOUS**
Glasslike (used to describe **luster**).

INDEX

USEFUL ADDRESSES

Gemological Institute of America
1660 Stewart Street, Santa Monica,
CA 9040, USA

American Gem Trade Association
181 World Trade Center, 2050 Stemmons
Expressway, Dallas, TX 75207, USA
www.agta.org

The Smithsonian Institute
Washington DC, 20560, USA
www.si.edu

International Colored Gemstones Association
609 Fifth Avenue, New York,
NY 10017

Canadian Gemmologist Appraisers Association
PO Box 69024, Vancouver, BC, V3K 4W3

Canadian Gemmological Association
21 Dundas Square, Suite 1209,
Toronto, Ontario,
M5B 1B7

Gemmological Association of Great Britain
27 Greville Street, London, EC1N 8TN
www.gagtl.ac.uk

The Gemmological Association of Australia
PO Box 14008, Melbourne City Mail Centre,
Victoria, 8001,
Australia

ACKNOWLEDGMENTS

The author would like to thank the Mineralogy Department curatorial team at the Natural History Museum (Alan Hart, David Smith, Peter Tandy, Henry Buckley, Andrew Clark) and the team leader Dr. Robert Symes for their help in getting gem specimens to Harry Taylor in the Photographic Department; my husband, Robert, and daughters, Alice and Emily, for giving me time to work quietly in my study, with only a few interruptions; Dr. Roger Harding, Alan Jobbins, Dr. Joseph Peters, and Christine Woodward for their expert help; and the team at Dorling Kindersley, especially Alison Edmonds, Alison Shackleton, Jonathan Metcalf, Mary-Clare Jerram, Lesley Malkin, and Lucinda Hawksley.

Dorling Kindersley would like to thank: Michael Allaby for compiling the index; Caroline Church for the endpapers; Neal Cobourne for the jacket design; Peter Bull for the rock cycle diagram 12 (tr); Janos Marffy for all additional artwork; Julia Pashley for picture research; Harry Taylor for his patience and co-operation during photography; Alastair Wardle for gem diagrams and the map on pp.14–15; Alison Edmonds for the loan of diamond jewelry for photography, 55 (cl); R. Keith Mitchell for the loan of taaffeite for photography 80 (t); Lesley Malkin and Constance Novis for additional editorial assistance; Peter Cross, Ann Thompson, and Kevin Ryan for additional design assistance.

All specially commissioned photography by Harry Taylor, except 11 (tr), 12 (cl), 13 (tr), 17 (bl & br), 18 (br), 19 (cl), 21 (cl), 26 (cutting a brilliant), 27 (br), 28 (tl & tr), 33 (tl, tr, bl, & br), 34 (tr, bl, & br), 35 (br), 36 (tl, cl & cr), 48 (c & bl), 50 (t & br), 55 (br), 57 (tl), 60 (br), 63 (tr & br), 67 (bl), 68 (cr), 69 (tr & br), 70 (cr & br), 71 (cl, cr, & br), 72 (cr), 74 (cl), 76 (bc), 77 (cl & cr), 78 (br), 81 (br), 82 (br), 83 (br), 85 (br), 87 (tc), 88 (bl & br), 92 (tr, tl, & bl), 93 (tr & c), 94 (br), 95 (cr & c), 98 (tr), 100 (br), 101 (tcr), 104 (tr), 106 (br), 107 (cr), 109 (tr), 110 (br), 112 (br), 113 (br), 117 (bl), 120 (tl, tr, & cl), 124 (bl), 125 (tr, cl, bl, & br), 130 (cl, cr, & br), 134 (c), 135 (bc), 138 (br), 139 (l), 141 (cl), 142 (bl & br), 143 (tl), 145 (cl, cr, bl, & br), 148 (br) by Colin Keates; 30 (tr) by Dave King; and 144 (t, bl, & br) by Matthew Ward.

The publishers would like also to thank the following for permission to reproduce their photographs and illustrations:
Vicky Ambery-Smith 50 (tl); Asprey Ltd 31 (br),

49 (cl); Bridgeman Art Library 57 (tc); Cartier 27 (tr), 29 (tr); Crown Copyright (reproduced by permission of the Controller of Her Majesty's Stationery Office) 7 (tr); De Beers 13 (bl & br), 14 (cl); Garrard, the Crown Jewellers 49 (br), 55 (t); Andrew Farmer 28 (bl); Michael Holford 11 (r), 31 (tr), 32 (c & tr), 59 (tc), 106 (br); The Hutchison Library 8 (br); Alan Jobbins 6 (tr), 8 (c), 15 (tr & bl), 20 (cr), 24 (br), 25 (tl, cr, & br), 32 (cr), 35 (cr), 36 (tr & br), 37 (tr), 56 (tr), 59 (tr), 60 (tr), 62 (tr), 75 (tr & cl), 82 (tr), 86 (bl), 94 (tr & cl), 135 (cr & br), 140 (tr), 145 (tr); Bernd Munsteiner 2, 29 (br); The Natural History Museum 11 (bl), 13 (cr), 21 (br), 23 (tr), 24 (bl), 38 (tl); The Platinum Advisory Centre 26 (br), 53 (tl & br)/Nicolas Sapieha 53 (tr); The Smithsonian Institution 76 (tr), 94 (cr), 107 (tr); Tiffany & Co 51 (tr & br), 55 (cr); The Victoria & Albert Museum 31 (cl), 32 (br), 125 (cr); Werner Forman Archive 30 (cr); The Worshipful Company of Goldsmiths 49 (tr), 50 (bl), 51 (bl & cr), 53 (bl).